Public Service Announcements

Rambling thought to help you in this complex world

KENNETH J. STANLEY, MD

ISBN: 1530472504
ISBN 13: 9781530472505
Library of Congress Control Number: 2016905577
CreateSpace Independent Publishing Platform
North Charleston, South Carolina

To God, who gave me the best parents a person can have.
To my parents, Rev. Jakie and Mrs. Nelsonia Stanley, who gave me
right back as soon as possible. Thank you for putting up with me
and for doing the best with what you had. There's a reason all my
high-school, college, and med-school friends still ask about you guys.

INTRODUCTION

Public Service Announcements is a compilation of my Facebook posts from 2010 to 2016. During this time my grandmother passed away, I got a divorce, changed jobs, got remarried, lost 30+ pounds, ran a marathon, watched a ton of sporting events, and attended hundreds of band performances, dance practices, football practices, soccer practices, basketball practices and some other stuff I left out. I wrote these thoughts down as an outlet- the way most of use social media. Most of them are funny, some of them are poignant. Because I am a doctor, many of the entries are medically themed. I hope you enjoy reading these and have a good laugh.

1

Here we go.

My wife and I pay $20 to park close to the finish line. I don't feel like paying, but I think that decision saves our lives.

Soon we are at the starting line. We're nervous and ready. I'm kidding—we were not ready, but we didn't know that. My goal was to finish in under 4 hours.

> Mile 1: Doing well, enjoying downtown Houston. Life. Is. Good.
>
> Mile 2: Focused, keeping a good pace, yet relaxed and in the moment. I tell myself I will remember as much of this as possible.
>
> Mile 4: Doing around eight minutes and forty-five seconds per mile. Could be going faster, but I'm pacing myself. Going to finish strong.

Mile 5 or 6: Pass Luke's Locker, the store where I buy my running gear. I happily wave to the people who put me in position to run.

Mile 8: Running by Rice University! So proud. (Side note—my wife and I went to Rice. *Go Owls! Woo! Yeah!*)

Mile 8.5: I gotta pee.

Mile 8.75: I gotta pee now!

Mile 9: Relief. Aaaahhhhh.

Mile 9: I should have locked that door.

Mile 9: I still haven't locked that door.

Mile 10: Starting to feel the miles, but I've been there before.

Mile 12: Some dude says I'm halfway done. I think he's bad at math.

Mile 13.1: Halfway home in under two hours. I. Am. A. *Stud!*

Mile 14: Keeping pace. Adrenaline is kicking in.

Mile 16: Not keeping pace. People are starting to pass me, and my legs kinda hurt. No biggie— I got this. Thinking three fifty.

Mile 17: The Wall is coming at mile 20. I am prepared. I've carb loaded and hydrated. Running a nice nine-fifteen pace. Nothing to be ashamed of.

Mile 18: I see something approaching. Oh my God—the Wall is coming for me. I try to swerve, but it just jumps on my back. "Howdy, pardner!"

Mile 18.4: I walk for about 0.4 miles. The Wall leaves.

Mile 19: The Wall comes back, with his friends the Gorilla and the Piano. Instead of me hitting the Wall, the Wall is hitting me.

Mile 19: I see dead people. Apparently they are a humorous lot, as they are laughing at me and all the other runners.

Mile 20: *Ouch!* My body has just gotten sore. I realize the guy at mile 12 may have been right. I am running but not really. My pace is around twelve minutes a mile. Three hours down. I am not making four hours.

Mile 21: I am mentally sending hate mail to Luke's Locker. I am considering returning my degree from Rice—wrapping it around a turd.

Mile 21.5: And now I gotta poop.

Mile 21.6: Spot a porta-potty. And in rushes a six-foot-four triathlete. He looks like Hercules but somehow larger. The porta-potty was trembling in fear as he was approaching. As he is dropping a Texas-size whopper in there, a seismologist at the University of Somewhere Very Far Away notes that an earthquake has registered 15.3 on the Richter scale in Houston. The Gorilla on my back actually runs away in fear. The poop in my bowels, now afraid, promises to behave as long as I do not go in that porta-potty.

Mile 21.7: I figure the dehydration will keep me from pooping.

Mile 22: Spectators are cheering. I'm so tired, so sore, and so appreciative I start to cry. Which keeps me from breathing. Crying ceases quickly as my survival instinct kicks in. Pain is leaving my body so that intense pain can come in. At this point, I realize how lucky *and* blessed I am to be in this position. I decide to enjoy the scenery and talk to strangers.

Mile 23: I run past a little girl trying to get a high five. Everyone is passing her because she is tiny. She doesn't realize this. She looks sad. So I turn around to give her a high five. And *holy cow*, my right arm hurts. Why has that happened!?!? Is she that X-Men character who creates pain when you touch her? Holy cow! She'd better be inspired to cure cancer or something. She smiles, her mom waves, and I begin to tear up and then suffocate and then keep running.

Mile 24: I ask the dude next to me where we are. He doesn't know either.

Mile 25: *I'm going to make it.* The Piano gets off.

Mile 26: The Wall wishes me good luck and leaves.

At this point, I get a surge of energy and emotion. I actually run across the finish line and get my medal.

Afterward, everything hurts!!! And gravity replaces the Wall because it takes me about a month to get up after having been seated. Christina has finished her half marathon. She greets me, we hug, and we trudge to the car, which is parked really close by.

Postscript: Two years later, I went to the marathon as a spectator with my daughter and one of her friends. We ate doughnuts. In my defense, I'd run four miles that morning. But, yeah, I took doughnuts to a marathon.

2

The number one benefit to having an 11 year old son- you save a lot of money on soap. I have no idea how he gets in the shower and comes out as dirty as he was when he got in, but he does it. Judging by the trail of ash, we have also saved on lotion.

3

Gravy is not a vegetable.

4

When it comes to politics in America, there are two groups of people: (1) people who threaten to move to Canada if their candidates lose and (2) those of us who will gleefully help the expatriates pack. Apparently *Canada* is Spanish for "whiny American refugee camp."

5

One of the advantages of driving a Ford F 250 Super Duty is that it is minimally damaged in an accident. Keep that in mind when you are texting while driving. In a school zone. And you drive a minivan. And since your main concern is not getting a ticket- your Nobel Peace Prize is in the mail.

6

Attorney Jim Adler extols his virtues and services in commercials, calling himself "the Texas Hammer." I think doctors should do the same thing. Therefore, please start referring to me as "the Diabetes Puncher." Dermatologists can be "Eczema Erasers"! A cardiologist can be "the Coronary Avenger of Justice and Mercy." I'll refrain from nicknaming gynecologists, urologists, and gastroenterologists.

7

Breath mints. For the love of God, please use them.

8

It is a good idea for you to use your car's turn signal when making a right-hand turn. It is an even better idea for you to use the right lane to make said turn. Since your turn signal is not a command to other drivers, your mean mugging, cursing, and pop-and-lock gesticulation will not magically move my car so you can cut off the car behind me. By the way, if you're going to risk your car and life, it had better be for a better reason than your trying to get to Chili's. I hope your life is worth more than oversalted potato skins.

9

It is important for you to look at prices while grocery shopping. We would all prefer that you compare prices before you get to the self-checkout lane. Since the prices are noted at the locations where you picked up said items, talking over the self-checkout is not necessary. On a related note, attempting to negotiate your own price for cereal and milk is not the most effective way to earn reward points, especially since the checkout machine cannot actually hear you.

10

If you are at an indoor trampoline park and your six-year-old is injured, walk up to him with your stroller filled to the brim with babies and say the following:

> "Stay here and watch the babies. Don't go anywhere."

A child is never too young to learn responsibility, even when he is too injured to carry out said responsibility. In his defense, he did stay right there.

11

Sometimes you go to the store and just forget what your wife told you to buy. No worries—just call her up, and ask what to pick up. Since it will still be in stock while you talk to her, it is OK to move out of the way of the four of us just trying to collect the items on our lists. Or even just get your cart out of the middle of the aisle so we can get by. Although I can tell you are upset that others want to do such rude things as pick up items or walk past you, I would like to remind you that your phone still works, lists can help, and no animals will be harmed by your moving approximately sixteen inches to let four people go about their business.

12

Mariah Carey is an amazing singer. You are singing along to one of her songs. You have the words in the right order. You do not have the notes in the right order. Therefore you are not Mariah Carey.

13

New Year's Eve 2015 in Houston—featuring the B-52s. Because apparently every other band was booked. We could have had local talent like Bun B, Beyoncé, or Katy Perry. I'm sure Michael from *Good Times* is available. Even my dog Fancy is more entertaining.

14

When I have the opportunity to see beautiful things, I am inspired to keep the memory intact by taking a picture. Specifically, taking a picture of the beautiful thing. And although I am a beautiful thing, I don't travel to take pictures of me.

15

Whenever someone says, "I'm not prejudiced, but…" expect to hear something prejudiced. For instance, I walked into my office after lunch today, and a new patient was in the waiting room. After I walked by and politely said, "Hello," the person asked my receptionist if I was the doctor. After being told I was indeed the doctor, the patient said, "I'm not prejudiced or anything like that, but is he, um, black?"

After being informed that the black person who'd just walked by is black, the patient called a family member and quickly left the office, leaving behind some medications and without getting a co-payment refund.

Should I have claimed to have reverse vitiligo? Or should I have gone with a freak tanning-bed-accident story? Next time this comes up, I'm going to say I'm Italian or Chinese just to see the look on the person's face.

16

I apologize for taking up some of the time you spend eating breakfast and watching the news, but your car keeps drifting into different lanes. Although you do have good dexterity and quick reflexes, I would appreciate it if you watched the road before nearly hitting that semi, minivan (with six passengers), and building.

17

Starting your day with exercise is good for your health and well-being. The best things about early exercise are the quiet streets, lack of traffic, and the fact that there is no one to see if you happen to trip and fall. I said "if." The one drawback is that it is hard to see anthills. The ants were *not* happy, allegedly.

18

Do not store your ChapStick next to your glue stick.

19

If you decide to wear a sheer skirt, pair it with nonsheer under-garments. Especially on a windy day.

20

When preparing for a half marathon, it is important for you to buy the right equipment and supplies. Since chafing can be an issue, Body Glide is an excellent product to buy. Today my nipples realized that just buying it is not enough. Also, it is not that cold here, I'm not *that* excited to see you, and I am not going to wear the finisher's medal on my chest at any time ever.

21

Give a man Viagra, and he will protect it with his life. It will be kept in a sealed vault that can be opened only with a code using cuneiform, hieroglyphics, the African clicking dialect, and pig latin. Give a man a Xanax, and it will be lost or stolen by two dudes within milliseconds. And he will ask for refills. Even from people who are not his doctor. Even from people who are not doctors.

22

If you are running a restaurant with the words "prime rib" in the name, you should have prime rib on the menu and, at least occasionally, on a plate. Or change the name of the place to Side Dishes, Empty Plates, or 78 Percent Nitrogen.

By the way, about twenty years ago, I went to Taco Bell one night, and they were out of tacos. They offered lettuce and sauce. I declined their full-price less-than-generous offer. I should have asked for a bell instead.

23

If I were the president of these here United States of America, right here, right now, in 2016, I would declare that the state of the Union is…Ohio! Take a bow! Then I'd sit down. Because whether you are a Republican, Democrat, Libertarian, Green, or Independent, you just don't want to listen to any speech longer than twenty-two seconds.

24

Star Wars movie spoiler: they're gonna make another Star Wars movie after this one.

25

When you see a new physician, it helps to bring your current medications to the office. Bringing them in pill bottles is the best way for the staff to identify the medications. Especially when you put the medications in the bottles that correspond to said medications. Although a Crown Royal bag will hold your medications, this is not recommended as the current standard of care.

26

September is Childhood Cancer Awareness Month. According to Facebook-arguing logic, if you do not post something about this, you do not care about kids with cancer, or you are in favor of kids having cancer.

27

When you go to an ER, it is OK if you let the ER staff begin to evaluate you before calling your PCP. This is valid advice, even when the staff tells you that they will call your PCP once they have evaluated you. I apologize in advance for not knowing the results of labs that have not been collected.

28

Another celebrity is under fire for making a racist statement. He has now released control to God (I am paraphrasing). I would suggest giving control to God all the time. Especially right before making really racist statements. On a related note, God is likely tired of being pinned to racism, drunkenness, marital infidelity, petty crime, sexual assault, and anything else that causes people to want public forgiveness. Leave it in God's hands, and then volunteer at a food bank instead of dropping N-bombs. OK?

29

Sakura Japanese Restaurant in Pearland has excellent service. The waitstaff is both accommodating and agile. A special thanks to the large group that congregated in front of the kitchen; oblivious to their surroundings, they created a perfect obstacle course for the waitstaff. Bonus points for getting the most asses in my wife's face for their group photo. We are honored to have been an ignored part of your celebration.

30

People: can't live with 'em, can't legally shoot 'em.

31

Just a reminder—I am eligible for the NFL draft.

32

Your mobile device can be set to deliver a silent alert. This means that when you receive a call or a text, the rest of us are not awakened during this conference. Even your flip phone has that feature.

33

If there is one thing that I learn at medical-education conferences, it's that highly educated people think that comb-overs and bad dye jobs are fooling someone. Besides themselves. I don't think they use mirrors.

34

It breaks my heart to hear about the death of a family pet. However, I am less sympathetic when the pet that died in the story six weeks ago died again last week. I would have been happy that Fido was resurrected. Did he eat your homework too?

35

Your legs can bend. Skinny jeans can bend. But if you can't bend your legs while wearing skinny jeans, your skinny jeans are too skinny.

36

If you're going to drive forty-five miles per hour on a freeway in Houston, Texas, while leaving your turn signal on for two miles, have fun with it! Make sure to show your passengers funny videos on your iPad while veering erratically from lane to lane. Point at the screen, laugh, gesticulate, administer high fives—all while impeding traffic. They say ignorance is bliss; thank you for sharing your bliss.

37

I am a forty-one-year-old male. Facebook is asking me what music I like. The choices displayed on my wall are Maroon 5, Linkin Park, and Taylor Swift. Based on this, I have clearly failed as a human being.

38

I have seen an online story about Ricki Lake claiming that marijuana can treat cancer. I have so many questions. Why does Ricki Lake's opinion matter? How is she still famous? Did someone get paid to ask Ricki Lake a health-related question? What does it say about society that it got published? Were all the doctors too busy for an interview? Did anyone blame Ebola yet? Was Sally Jessy Raphael somehow not available? Why does the media keep printing baseless speculations by uninformed quasi celebrities? Are we just out of news at this time? Like, did we run out of actual useful news?

39

It is legal to make a right turn on a red light if no traffic is coming. It is also legal to make a right turn on a green light. Yep, still legal. Just a reminder: Green. Means. Go.

40

Apparently there is a movie called *Frozen*. I wonder if it has a sound track.

41

Knowing what medications you take on a daily or weekly basis is a good way to take charge of your health. Knowing why you take said medications is also a good idea. Not telling your doctor (or his/her staff member) which medications you take or why is a bad idea. Getting offended when we ask keeps us on our toes, but it decreases the likelihood that we'll have any clue how to help you. I suggest seeing a psychic if you want the mind-reader package.

42

If you come to a margarita festival and pay for Bud Light, you get to drink Bud Light. That's why the line was shorter—and the sign said "Bud Light."

43

If the reigning NFL Defensive Player of the Year stops by your son's football practice, make sure you have memory on your phone before he starts talking. On a related note, I do not have proof that this happened, and J. J. Watt is a really nice guy.

44

Putting a magnetic sign on your car featuring the word ACCOUNTANT actually makes me less likely to trust you with my money.

45

If you can't master the concept of the drive-through ATM machine, your problems are not just financial. I'm not suggesting that you do not have money problems; I'm just pointing out that money is not your root problem. Shaking the machine works on some vending machines and pinball machines, not ATM machines. And peering in the slot where the money comes out works only if you are a Jedi. Finally, just for safety, bring a car to the drive-through lane.

46

Exactly two people have contracted Ebola during patient care. Two. Although this may turn into a pandemic here in the States, I just do not see where two patients is apocalyptic. There were around thirty cases of SARS, and people did not lose their minds and blame Canada for pestilence, famine, and halitosis. Before saying the CDC and the president are knuckle-dragging morons, let's calm down and see if science and medicine can work.

47

A lady came to my office after having passed out. She turned her head to the left and went down. She awoke in less than one minute. Her husband tried to help her, but she did not know what had happened. Therefore, the sequence of events was *turn, down, for what*!

48

Miley Cyrus does not listen to Miley Cyrus anymore. If you are a grown man and you are blasting Miley Cyrus music in public, just get help. Now.

Ms. Cyrus, I offer my sincere apologies if you do listen to your own music. I still think I am not the target demographic. I mean, that other guy is not your target demographic.

49

Asking your doctor for advice is generally a good idea. Sometimes I field questions that are not medical in nature. Yesterday I was asked career advice: What is the likely return on investment if one were to become a rapper versus an NBA player? Despite not being an expert in these affairs, I advised that both choices need good backup plans.

50

Since I have read Facebook posts on legal issues from the Hobby Lobby Supreme Court case to the Ray Rice case, I have come to one conclusion. Literally everyone is a lawyer. Constitutional, criminal, civil, intellectual property, civil rights—all of that. I'm just glad I do not work in a profession where people go to Google or watch TV commercials to tell me how to do my job that took seven years to get (after college).

51

If you go to a nice restaurant, do not assume the well-dressed black male is the valet. Unless you drive an Aston Martin. If you drive a car like mine, I am a doctor. If you drive an Aston Martin, I'm the valet.

52

Made Jiffy Pop popcorn. The kids were unimpressed. I need to get new kids.

53

The effectiveness of any given medical treatment is not affected by the fact that you have never heard of it. If that were true, literally no new treatment would ever work. Unless researchers told you about it first.

54

The next three all occurred within a span of ten minutes.

1. When traveling with young'uns, it is often necessary to stop at a gas station or truck stop to let Lil Timmy go potty. Please remember that the gas pump is not the actual restroom and a soda bottle is not the toilet. Feel free to help Lil Timmy learn what aim is. Just walk forty feet to use a restroom as a restroom. Especially when Lil Timmy is wearing Pull-Ups.

2. Once you have made it into the restroom to do number two: Lock. The. Door. Or answer when someone knocks to see if the stall is occupied. Granted, your cursing is effective in signaling that the stall is occupied, but the lock works too.

3. Yes, all at one truck stop. Extensions are normally a good way to get extra hair to make a look that people

find attractive. Not so much if you are a sixty-five-year-old male. With gray hair. And jet-black extensions. In your damned beard. And you braid the extensions and tie it all behind the back of your neck to make a ponytail. I need a beer and a cigarette. And I don't like beer—nor do I smoke.

55

Infants and toddlers love to go to playgrounds. And prepared parents bring diapers and extra sets of clothes. If your little one needs to be changed, it is perfectly acceptable to do it at the playground. However, I suggest that you move your child off the playground equipment. It is difficult for the other kids to avoid stepping on your kid. On a related note, your kid can have that slide all to himself.

56

When enjoying a beautiful public space, taking a picture will make the memory last a lifetime. Personally, I would aim the camera away from my face. Otherwise every beautiful place looks just like my face. Bonus points to the budding photographer for blocking the sidewalk and getting upset about stepping in a mud puddle that he didn't see because he'd been looking at himself.

57

Corresponding with your clients is an important part of any business. Making yourself available via e-mail or text messaging adds a personal touch. When responding to messages, I highly recommend hitting "Send" to make the message really hit home.

58

To the person who looked both ways before crossing the street and darted out in front of my oncoming car anyway, I'm sorry that my decision to go forward offended you. I guess green means go only if Your Highness approves. I am impressed by the protective powers of your middle finger and pouty lips. Instead of offering one-gun salutes while playing Frogger, why not just wait until you have the right-of-way?

59

Jogging is a great way to exercise. Jogging with friends adds additional benefits. For instance, if you and your friends run in a formation that blocks the running trail, you get to play red rover. Or chicken. This is good for developing quick reflexes.

60

One drawback to being a physician is that I receive junk e-mail from Republicans. One drawback to being African American is that I get junk e-mail from Democrats. Neither party will get a donation from me, because they keep addressing me as Kevin.

61

When you're attending your child's dance recital, I recommend that you use the theater seats as seats. Using the aisle as a seat or using the seat as an aisle or ladder is counterproductive, especially when someone is occupying the seat in question. On a completely related note, do not act surprised when your alternative arrangement ends with an injury.

62

When your health provider advises you to drink plenty of fluids, please note that alcohol, gravy, and syrup are not the ideal fluids for recuperation. And by syrup, I mean both maple and sizzurp.

63

If the word for "more than one octopus" is *octopi* and the word for "more than one platypus" is *platypi*, then the word for "more than one apple" is *apple pie*.

64

(on Father's Day)

I would like to thank my kids. Without them, I would not be a father.

65

Fellas, if you're going to jog or go to the gym, wear pants. Speedos are not pants. If you must wear a Speedo (and remember—you must not), wear a color that is noticeably different from your own skin color. And if you still cannot avoid looking nude, do your stretching at home. Please.

66

Hang up and drive, especially while eating with utensils.

67

Apparently I have been doing my job wrong for the last thirteen years. I should have been prescribing tea tree oil for every malady and affliction. A person who asked for my medical advice has used this for all his symptoms and is demanding that I tell all my patients about it. None of his symptoms are getting better, but that did not stop him from informing me that FDA-approved medications, supplements, and magic potions cannot approximate the healing power of tea tree oil. With one exception—Viagra.

68

We do not have a Viagra-dispensing machine at my office. The fact that you have been to my office before is not a guarantee that we'll give you samples of Viagra. Or even a prescription. Or even the name of a doctor who just hands out Viagra to people who demand it from the magic Viagra tree. But thank you for the offer to let us serve your needs for free.

69

When you write an amorous text to your spouse, send the text to your spouse.

70

Orange wig, see-through skintight white T-shirt with a pink bra, C cups in a B-cup holder, tramp stamp, gold sandals, and stretch pants stretched to their finite and transparent limit. Yep, I am at Chuck E. Cheese's.

71

A car's turn signal is an important safety feature. It is meant to alert your fellow drivers that you will be changing lanes or turning. It is not intended to be a warning that you're about to take immediate evasive action because you *need* to go across three lanes of Houston freeway traffic to get to Starbuck's / McDonald's / your girl's place while on your phone. It is not a "do what I want now" excuse card. Unless you are an action hero. You are not an action hero.

72

Once again, I am waiting by the phone, waiting on an NFL team to call. No other draft prospect has my exact combination of size, speed, strength, skill, or alliterative prose. If I can't make the show, who can?

73

If you are a specialist physician, it is important that you document symptoms the patient tells you, even when they are not related to your field of expertise. That being said, when a neurologist documents that a patient has no menstrual abnormalities, I am suspicious that this issue came up in conversation. I am not surprised this patient has no menstrual abnormalities, because he lacks adequate menstrual equipment. Despite the fact that the patient's gynecologic exam was documented as normal, I do not think it was very gynecologic.

74

(after Los Angeles Clippers owner Donald Sterling was forced to sell his team following his racist remarks to his mistress, asking her why she was hanging out with Magic Johnson) I am glad racism is over. I can't wait to attend an NBA game with the mistress of the team owner. I'm thankful that I am alive to see the realization of Dr. Martin Luther King's vision. We have truly overcome.

75

Deaf people cannot hear. Therefore, talking louder only makes the rest of us jealous of the deaf person. Also, there is more to sign language than pointing at things while grunting. If there is a hell, the entertainment there would be having to play charades with you.

76

(after receiving a check for $0.00 at my office) There are many different ways to reward people. A check with a lot of zeros is a great reward. But only if there is a positive number in front of the zeros. I promise not to spend it all in one place. Or anyplace.

77

Sometimes in life, unfortunate things happen. Sometimes we have to get over it and move on. I'm going out on a limb here, but saying, "Don't worry; you'll get over it," is not an appropriate response when someone tells you her husband of sixty-five years just died. However, the newly minted widow's reply of "You're right! I am sooo over it. I should have thought of that!" made my smart-alecky heart smile. We definitely shared a moment. Sometimes humor is the best medicine.

78

Quote of the Day So Far

"You're not a gynecologist, right? You're an MD." His next request was for Xanax. I decided not to prescribe Xanax.

79

Your March Madness / Final Four / NCAA Men's Basketball tournament bracket will be in shambles after the second day. So will mine. All of us will be able to go on in life without hearing your eloquent expressions of the turmoil and sadness you have encountered because of the loss of twenty dollars. Somewhere a child soldier in Sudan or a homeless man in your own hometown weeps for your anguish.

80

(After a group of white supremacists held up a Diversity = White Genocide sign) I am a proponent of "diversity." I am not a proponent of "genocide." I am a proponent of using a "dictionary."

81

Applying cologne before a night out is a good way for you to enhance your social appeal. However, there is a law of diminishing returns. If small animals pass out when you walk by, you may have taken this too far. Also, none of us have been chopping onions or had a death in the family. But all of our eyes are watering.

82

Ebola and *uvula* are not synonyms.

83

Just because a dress is strapless, doesn't mean it does not need to stay up.

84

You know how people who win Oscars and Grammys thank their lovely spouses? If you marry an ugly person, are you automatically ineligible for a major award? If so, I'd like to apologize to my lovely wife for making her ineligible to win an Oscar.

85

If you are at the rodeo and you want to sing along to the song with someone but you are not sure of the words, don't pick the black guy. He is not able to help.

86

(to the insurance company that faxed a patient's glucose diary to my office on Friday, February 21, 2014 at 9:04 p.m.)
Thank you for sending my patient's glucose diary from July and August 2013. Good communication helps me to serve patients better. Now let's aim for timely communication.

This patient had actually brought the same glucose diary to an office visit in August 2013. So, yeah, not the best use of resources.

87

Bicycle riding is a great source of exercise. Be safe and wear a helmet. Especially when riding around aimlessly. In Target. While leaving your poorly behaved kids behind.

88

If your cousin keeps stealing your medications, you should not keep putting them in the same place. Or stop lying to me in an effort to get a prescription. Or keep lying, but change the story to keep me off base. Or just stop. That's it. Just stop.

Drug addiction is a serious problem, and prescription-medication diversion is a major public-health issue. I was expressing my frustration at this moment. It's part of the job, but the issues doctors deal with pale in comparison to the issues that patients have with drug abuse. And some of the patients who have drug-abuse issues are doctors too.

89

Take the extra time and effort to write out the words "Valentine's Day." Because no one ever had a "Happy VD." Someone may have had fun getting there, but that is beside the point.

90

Hot flashes due to menopause do not cause pneumonia. If that were true, most women in their fifties would constantly have pneumonia.

Seriously, people, learn to apply common sense before applying cause and effect to your situation. Just because two things happen at the same time, do not think one thing caused the other.

91

(to the man I saw leaving a public restroom) Wiping your hands with a dry paper towel is not the same as washing your hands. Do you change a baby's diaper by literally just changing the diaper? Although I appreciate your looking guilty and uttering the bacteria-killing phrase "My bad," I would prefer that you employ the time-honored ritual of my people—using soap and water.

92

If I were president, my State of the Union address would go as follows: "My fellow Americans, this year's state of the Union is…Delaware!!! Good night, and God bless America!"

I'd just pick a state at random, say the name really loudly, and leave to thunderous applause, because no matter what I say, someone will clap like a circus seal. At least my speech will be over quickly, and the rebuttals would be short too. Then next year, everyone would see whether his or her state would become the state of the Union.

93

(for Houstonians who watch the TV news reports when the temperature gets into the midthirties) Apparently all the freeways will become glaciers. We should also watch out for marauding bands of polar bears, penguins, and icebergs. Yes, icebergs will attack you. And they will give you lice. According to the news reports.

94

If you bring a loved one to a physician's office, it is reasonable to let said physician perform the physical exam. Most physicians do better exams when they do the actual examining themselves. I am impressed that you know medical terms. I'd be more impressed if you knew how to use those terms in a complete sentence. Or if you knew how to make a complete sentence.

95

If you are a burgeoning songwriter, you may feel that artistic license allows for swear words. Please remember that you can use other words as well. Your normal word / F-bomb ratio should be greater than 3:1. At least try another word. Even a different curse word would be an improvement.

96

If you are going to claim that you heal people with the power of touch, you should expect people to doubt you. People who doubt you are not necessarily minions of Satan or "the devil," as you have said. We just don't buy what you are selling. You longingly wish that others could have the healing experience you provide. People with terminal illnesses want cures. I see a matchmaking opportunity here. Get to healing, and I will start to following. Seriously, if you are on Facebook or Twitter claiming you have healed multiple people in public (for *free*!!!), I bet one of them would friend or follow you and passionately back you up.

97

Flesh-toned, skintight leggings should not be paired with a skin-baring top. At least I hope those were leggings.

98

If you are in a meeting and you *must* talk to your neighbor while the speaker is speaking, try to whisper. And by "try," I mean "succeed." If everyone in the room turns and shoots you a death glare, it's time to learn sign language, semaphore, or telepathy. Or learn to not talk.

99

If you are a politician and you are asked about slavery, the correct answer is "I'm against it." Unless you are volunteering to be an actual slave. If you say you would allow slavery because it is the will of your constituents, then I will move to your district and start a grassroots petition for you to not only become a slave but get a sex-change operation against your will. Remember—slavery is bad. You're welcome.

100

Nothing says "Donate to the Salvation Army" more than an NFL halftime show on Thanksgiving. Especially when the show consists of a scantily clothed lip-sync artist. Now I am going to donate to United Way instead.

101

Under normal circumstances, wearing clothes that match is a good idea. An exception is when you wear see-through pants. The Houston Texans appreciate your visible show of support.

102

A doctor prescribing a medication will not cure your condition—especially when you don't bother to take said medication. Holding a prescription in your hand is clinically proven to not work at all. I would like to heal you with my gracious touch or lofty gaze, but I skipped that day of class. Fortunately your pharmacist awaits.

103

Duct tape—works every time.

104

To the weight-loss doctor who came to my office today—I admire your willingness to meet other medical professionals. That's a great way to get referrals and drive business to your office. And thanks for the chocolate chip cookies; making me and my staff fatter will help to provide more patients for you. Were you out of biscuits and gravy? Am I supposed to take you seriously at this point?

105

Texting while driving is a bad idea. That being said, doing so while your phone is exactly two inches from your eyes adds an extra degree of difficulty. Thank you for allowing me to practice my evasive maneuvers. And way to barely avoid that three-story building that suddenly came out of nowhere.

106

With today's charged political climate, political rallies and protests are common. Here's some helpful advice to help you make your desired impact. Make your sign readable. There is a reason artists do not use dark paint on a dark background. Also, use legible writing. Calligraphy is beautiful, but no one can read it. Finally, if you have a catchy chant, try saying it together. "Hasha Frasha wha-wha-wha" worked for Scooby, Shaggy, and Charlie Brown's teacher. But it ain't working for you.

107

When your fake lips are almost as big as your fake breasts, you should not wear enough bright red lipstick to make you look like a Kabuki warrior. Circus clowns are subtler.

108

When a stranger of your ethnicity walks up to you and says, "I'm not trying to be racist," you can rest assured that he or she will succeed in being racist.

The best part- he complained about Mexicans to me, a guy who is married to a Mexican.

109

Thank you for telling me that all I need to prescribe for your illness is "the little round white pill." Armed with this new information, I will hastily switch all my patients to this medication. I can't believe that pharmacies bother to stock nonwhite, nonround pills. Or capsules. I am getting a refund from my medical school for this egregious lack of instruction. Note: no one will be getting Dilaudid or "the little blue pill," because they are no longer necessary.

110

Drive-through services are for people with cars. A baby stroller is not a car. So please fasten the safety belt for your toddler, put out your cigarette, and walk into the building to do your business. I look forward to hearing about you in a Darwin Awards book.

111

When a product container tells you not to put that product in your ear, do not put that product in your ear. Also, do not try to convince anyone that you did not put that product in your ear, especially after it was found in your ear, removed from your ear, and shown before your eyes.

112

I just heard a song by Shabba Ranks on the radio. Any time I get all judgmental about new music or another musical genre, I am reminded of the oily skinned, facially challenged, unintelligible-word-using crooner's chart-topping success. And I have to deal with the guilt and regret that I was partially responsible. It makes me wish I had used drugs so I'd have an excuse.

113

If you find yourself stranded because of car trouble, you need to get your car fixed. If you want to accomplish that goal, do not do the following: yell incomprehensibly, take off your shirt, stomp around your car, mean mug, growl, or pimp slap your car. Being a topless male with a broken hand will not cause your car to realize its error and try to leave you. Unfortunately.

114

OK. The insurance company that recently sent my office a seventeen-cent check told a patient that I not only am no longer in their network but do not actually exist. When the patient tried to explain that he not only was in my office but had been there before, the befuddled insurance worker told him she would have to "check and see" if I existed. I hope I never need a letter of recommendation from her. At least I heard him tell her, "If I give you his fax number, is that an admission of his existence?" and "No, I do not know his social security number—why would I know that?"

115

If you decide to purchase $250 worth of wine from a grocery store, it is in no way, shape, or form acceptable for you to argue over a $3 coupon. Even if you do not understand the concept of "expired."

116

I promise not to "sweat" your "swag." In return, I request that you not sweat my "degree," "job," or "pants that cover my backside."

117

If you choose to show off your dance moves in public while playing "Dance-Off!!" at the local mall, you may want to add a bra to your ensemble. On a completely related note, I would sell my soul to anyone who would design and sell a man bra.

118

Sleeveless shirts are not attractive on all people. If your arms lack definition to the point that you cannot carry a dictionary, wear sleeves. If you sport a tattoo suggesting you are well endowed, wear sleeves. And if it looks like you have a rabid, sweating sheepdog in your armpit, use deodorant and wear sleeves.

And, yes, I qualify as someone who should never wear a sleeveless shirt.

119

Toothpaste is for teeth. Therefore, if you have a nontooth problem, do not apply toothpaste. And do not lend anyone your toothbrush.

120

There are times in life where a person has to be late for an appointment. That being said, requesting the first visit of the day, being forty-five minutes late, and saying "I want an x-ray" instead of "Hello" will not endear yourself to the patients who show up on time. And if the office does not have an x-ray machine, making your request louder will not make an x-ray machine magically appear. In order to meet your medical wishes, you must find the magic lamp, rub it, and talk to Aladdin directly. I do agree that diagnostic testing is needed for this person.

121

Occasionally I have forgotten my wallet and been without my insurance card, ID, and money. And I understand that can happen at any time. That being said, if the receptionist asks for your insurance card, responding by demanding free service because you forgot your wallet is not an effective strategy. Not only does my office not give discounts to people who forget to bring payment, but we can see your wallet in your back pocket. Good luck at Starbuck's or Walmart with that strategy.

122

I have been eligible for the NBA draft for more than twenty years. This last season alone, twenty-nine of the thirty teams that did not have me on their rosters did not win the NBA title. You would think someone would have noticed this trend and fixed this problem.

123

Bad, unintentional pun of the day: I told a patient with a stomach virus, "It's not a serious condition, but it will bug the crap out of you."

124

Some people have IQs that are negative integers. I not referring to people with problems like cerebral palsy or Alzheimer's. I'm talking about alleged grown-ups who may qualify for Darwin Awards. (This is what I posted. I guess I could have referred to doctors who have bad grammar or fathers who can't proofread as people with low IQ scores.)

125

When jogging in a public area, jogging forward is a good plan. There are no other good jogging plans. Just ask the guy who fell off his bike trying to avoid you. Oh, you can't—because you quickly ran off without rendering aid.

126

(to the insurance company that had me pulled from a patient visit to take a phone call from one of their doctors) I am glad that you have employed physicians who can read. Having a board-certified physician read questions from two forms I previously filled out has restored my faith in humanity, books, libraries, dictionaries, and grammar itself. Sure, this could have been handled by reading the forms silently to oneself or by reading aloud to other insurance-company employees. But taking the time to tell me what I already wrote makes me feel included in the decision-making process. Although I will never get those ten life-altering minutes of my life back, at least I have the comfort of knowing that people who finished grad school can read.

127

Usually it is a good idea for you to dress in a manner that highlights your best assets. That being said, it is never a good idea as a male to wear biking shorts as outerwear while jogging. Especially when transparent white is not your color, Mr. Jiggle Junk.

128

If you are a courier and you need to call your supervisor about an item we mislabeled, it is acceptable for you to use your inside voice and toothpaste. Once you have informed the office staff how to fix the problem, let it go. Telling us once or twice is helpful; spending ten minutes complaining to us about us with a booming tone that registers on the Richter scale is a tad bit excessive. Excuse me while I power wash my waiting room to recover from this encounter.

129

Here is how an eight-year-old ruins Superman: "If they knew the planet was going to be destroyed, why did they make only one escape pod? And why didn't they make it big enough for more than one baby?"

130

I love art, and in my opinion, Native American motifs are some of the most visually appealing. Unless applied to stretch pants being worn as outerwear. And please—if you make that fashion faux pas, stand up straight. I beg of you.

131

(to the man whose woman caused him disrespect during a phone conversation while at Kroger) There is a *t* at the end of *disrespect*. Not a *k*. Based on your conversation, raising your voice does not seem to be garnering any respeck. Nor does the use of your beloved F-bomb. Although your ability to maintain focus despite the stares and glares of your public is laudable, complaining about having your business in the streets while loudly putting your business in the streets seems self-defeating. I can't believe she let you go.

132

Your priorities are misplaced when you replace your car's back-seat with speakers and your child rides on the trunk. At least the trunk had a seat and a seat belt.

133

Rubber gloves are commonly used in medical practice. Interestingly enough, they are not often used as contraceptive devices or hair ties. Although I laud the creativity displayed, I cannot recommend these uses for rubber gloves.

134

(to the man wearing a Confederate flag T-shirt and a perfectly arranged black bow tie) Your fly is down. Oh, and did you look in the mirror and say, "I need to make this outfit complete. Should I go with the bow tie or cummerbund?" I bet he's available!

135

Sometimes we parents have to let our children learn from their mistakes. Actions have consequences. So if your teenager plows a car into another car, telling him to report that you are the driver is a bad idea. Asking the injured owner of the car your teenager just hit to corroborate your story is actually a next-level bad idea. Especially when you are not even at the scene of the accident.

136

I saw a billboard advertising a church's Easter program. To commemorate the death, burial, and resurrection of Jesus Christ, our Lord and Savior, this church is having a helicopter drop plastic eggs on children. That clearly falls under the WWJD rubric. Will they use a grenade launcher to show the power of the Lord? Apparently they couldn't find a jump jet. If Jesus came back and saw this, he would say, "I did *not* die for this!" or "I'm pretty sure you guys missed the point if this whole Bible thing." If anyone from this church complains about the secularization of Christmas, I'm going rent a helicopter and drop holiday trees, Festivus poles, and dreidels on the adults there.

137

My ability to guess your diagnosis with as little information as possible is not based on my education, attention, or relationship with whichever God you worship. Although this is a great premise for a game show, it is a lousy way for me to make sure you are not dying soon.

138

If you want me to tell you whether your prescription medication interacts with another medication, please tell me the name of the prescriptions you actually take. If you don't take the "one in that TV commercial," you have nothing to fear. Also, there's more than one "round white pill." I need more specifics—or training in paranormal activities.

139

Niagra is not the name of a prescription medication. Even when you show me a handwritten prescription for Niagra, I will not write you another prescription for Niagra. I do not think the prescription being shown to me is really for Niagra. And, no, I will not change the spelling on that prescription for you.

Sometimes patients steal prescription pads and try to write their own prescriptions. I'm pretty sure that's what happened in this case.

140

(to the lady wearing an interesting plaid skirt and top while sporting blond, neon-red, and orange hair with gray roots) Thank you for your tribute to Catholic schoolgirls. Turning the staid plaid outfit into a halter top was a bold decision. So is invading Russia in the winter, but still. The brightness and gaiety of your outfit made heads turn in both directions. Just remember—if you don't advertise, you don't sell. Although it would help to use a better marketing technique.

141

(to the lady mentally undressing me as I type this) Although I am flattered, your efforts have only succeeded in removing my libido. Your wedding ring indicates that this tactic may have worked with Mr. Creepy, but today ain't your day. I am prepared to fake my own death or use pepper spray to make you stop.

142

Hell is not a super hot place in the ethereal realm filled with torture and demons. Hell is a dance competition in a fifty-degree room populated by adults who think that shrieking like dying banshees who can survive only by clawing their fingernails into twelve thousand chalkboards while their scantily clad (and clumsy) seven-year-olds dance will lead to world peace or first prize. And said competition will have to be two hours behind schedule. If I see one more bedazzled-T-shirt-wearing adult give a child the stink eye for a substandard performance, so help me God, I am hiring a series of hit men for the adults and counselors for the kids.

143

I'm watching *The Bible* on History. All the characters have British accents. Guess it makes them sound more important. *Rome* (HBO) did the same thing. Just once I want to see a historical drama where all the characters have Canadian accents—eh? Or maybe Jamaican accents.

144

I believe that Jesus is omnipotent. He can do anything. That being said, he is not going to grant your weight-loss dreams through your current diet plan of gravy, pork, soda, and beer. Or your exercise regimen of jack squat. Even though Jesus has unlimited time and talent, he has better things to do than to make your forty-year-old self look like a twenty-five-year-old supermodel while eating enough calories to change the earth's rotation.

145

If there is one thing that all people have in common, it's the fact that eating a funnel cake on a windy day makes all of us look like we just finished a cocaine binge.

146

(to the man who was fired from his job after slapping a baby on an airplane flight) I just have one question (and then a rant): Who thinks slapping babies makes them **stop** crying? I mean, who says, "If I just slap Timmy, he will be happy and stop crying"? Does he think he has Jesus's healing touch? Are his hands so soft and supple that he has a history of infants saying, "Wow, that hurt, but your skin is so soft—what kind of lotion do you use?" And since when is a crying baby on an airplane a surprise? Just deal with it. I've heard that babies have a tendency to cry for a number of reasons. One of which is having been slapped in the face by a deranged stranger. Dimwit.

147

There are seven different versions of Crest Complete tooth-paste. And multiple versions of Crest Pro-Health, which I must assume is incomplete. But Complete is obviously for amateurs. I'm holding out for All-Star, Hall-of-Fame, All-Encompassing toothpaste...that is omniscient too.

148

A few observations from my daughter's dance competition: This is how God is getting me back for all of those three-day/all-day basketball tournaments. Some of these kids are really good. Put clothes on your damn kids. Dance keeps the make-up/hair-spray/sequin industry alive. Six in the morning is too early to dance or prance. Lyrical/jazz/musical theater—what is the difference, and why do they need different shoes for each type? I need Adderall. I appreciate our dance teachers. The level of estrogen in this room would suffocate my son. I would be OK if I could go home (any home). I am grateful for the opportunity to support my daughter. This is definitely worth it.

149

If there is a hell, the floor is a hard surface covered by small, overly caffeinated children in shiny new tap-dancing shoes.

150

One of my patients got a kidney transplant yesterday. "You don't appreciate urine until it's gone and it comes back." So true. Giving thanks for technology and people sacrificing to share the gift of life.

151

When opportunity knocks, be ready to answer the door. When an attractive lady catches your eye on Valentine's Day, impress her with a double-take stare. Bonus points if your mouth is wide-open. And make sure your physician is made aware of the attractive woman's presence while in the physician's office. Thank you.

152

Lifting weights at your local gym is a great way for you to stay in shape. Sitting on exercise equipment is a good start. May I suggest actually using the equipment? Checking your phone while sitting is not turning you into a Greek god. And monopolizing the machine for ten minutes while looking upset when asked to move can lead to injury. Thanks for finally taking that call while standing under a sign that says "Do not use mobile communication devices in the weight room."

153

If you have a physical abnormality like a heart murmur, it is a good idea for you to inform your primary-care physician. That being said, informing your PCP during the cardiac exam makes it difficult for him to hear said murmur. Especially when you shout.

154

That special moment when your children are playing together and talking quietly, sharing. And the next moment when you stop, listen, and hear them scientifically discuss how to figure out who farted in a large crowd.

155

For doctors: When you attend a meeting with a buffet-style dinner, use the tongs. Especially during a flu epidemic.

156

Men, it is important that you teach your sons good hygiene. That means you should let them see you wash your hands. Which means you should actually wash your hands. Make sure they wash their hands after using the restroom. Also, teach them that the scented disk in the urinal is not soap.

157

If you get winded having a bowel movement, it's time for you to consider an exercise regimen. If you get winded wiping, see a cardiologist first.

158

The next male to demand that I "Just prescribe a damn pill!" when I ask if he has had a fever or other symptoms will be getting a birth control pill.

159

Men, the Children's Museum of Houston is a great place to bring your daughters. Spending time with your daughters sends a strong message. Doing so while wearing a T-shirt proclaiming "My Bandz Can Make You Dance!" sends a conflicting message. Unless you are a choreographer. And I don't think this guy was a choreographer. Unless choreographers get paid in singles, because that's how he paid for his family's admission.

160

Because of the phenomenon known as antibiotic resistance, sometimes a prescribed antibiotic will be ineffective. That being said, the fact that you are not cured of your pneumonia within three seconds of inhaling the fumes from the prescription bottle is not a sign that antibiotic resistance has occurred. Calling your physician or pharmacist immediately will not make the antibiotic more potent. Please remember—medical professional does not equal magician.

161

The number-one reason why I have problems at work: I am still employed.

162

If you are spending Christmas morning standing in front of a convenience store smoking a cigarette and drinking coffee, you are loitering. The police are not harassing you. Especially when you are loitering in front of the No Loitering sign.

163

If you are reading this post, then you have survived your second apocalypse within the last year. I keep hearing about people who buy supplies to be prepared for these apocalypses (*apocalypsae?*). What supplies do you need if life is going to end? No one will collect on that life-insurance policy. Flame-retardant clothes are not space suits; therefore a lack of planet Earth renders them useless. That fire extinguisher you got at Walmart is not going to put out a volcano raining down fire and brimstone. And your guns are useless against large comets and meteors. Unless you are an Egyptian pharaoh, you do not plan on taking your belongings with you to the afterlife. And if you really think this is the wrath of God, what in God's name are you going to buy that will stop the Almighty? Better keep that receipt.

164

One day, a man brought his wife to my office because she was ill. He happened to be wearing a baseball cap with a Confederate flag and the word REBEL on it. When I walked in the room, he realized that he was wearing a potentially offensive cap. I say "potentially" because the embarrassed look on his face nearly made me fall over laughing. If you're embarrassed to wear certain clothes around certain people (like your personal physician), consider other clothing options.

165

I think most of us agree that tobacco use is bad for your health. At no point in time have I advised anyone to dip snuff while smoking. They do not cancel each other out. Also, you know it's time to quit when your doctor's office has to buy more Lysol and air-conditioner filters after each visit. Those were not tears of joy, my friend.

166

(noted on December 6, 2012) I AM the most compassionate doctor, according to American Registry, LLC. I just got a fax, so it must be true. And for $109.00 (plus $12.90 shipping and handling), I can get a plaque saying I am a most compassionate doctor for 2011. Not a typo—last year. I guess I've been more vile this year. Anyone with this plaque in his or her office may also be the most narcissistic doctor ever.

167

If you are going to lip-synch your way through an NBA half-time performance or concert, get a wireless-headphone-type mic. Or just remember to hold the mic near any body part. I'm good either way. And if (when) you forget the words to the songs, consider moving your lips. At least try to fool me.

168

(posted on Thanksgiving Day after the 2012 election) At this special time of year, as truly blessed Americans, we can find common ground and transcend any political differences we may have and come together for a common cause. We all agree that it is time for you to take the Obama or Romney sign off your lawn. If you have neighbors, friends, or relatives who have not done so, assist them by removing each sign and replacing it with either a Romney or Obama sign. Or any other sign of your choosing. Be creative. I'm thinking Garage Sale or Solicitors Welcome!

169

I realize many people want to treat their hypertension, obesity, or diabetes "naturally," meaning without the use of medications. I would like to do the same thing for my patients. Therefore, I propose the following: exercise. It's all-natural—unlike the diet pill you just asked about or the supplement your friend who has not lost weight has suggested. Seriously, if you spend all your time not moving, how am I magically going to cure you? And your repeatedly asking me how to not eat right or exercise your way to good health will not convince the heart attack to go away, no matter how sincere you are. I'd suggest eating healthily, but the McDonald's bag tells me this message will fall on deaf ears. And stop asking for a miracle. God does not exist so that your fifty-year-old self can eat Whoppers and gravy all day and still look hot in a bikini. He could pull that off, but he's been busy trying to get you to exercise instead.

170

(to the man with the late-1990s' candy-colored Lincoln Continental with the eighteen-inch rims) Wait—how do I know they are eighteen-inch rims? Because the custom-made wheel well said "18 inch rims." Thank you. By the way, nice touch with the TVs in the backseat headrests. I love SpongeBob too.

171

If you let your eleven-year-old child. wear a shirt that says "Certified Rain Maker," you'd better be a Native American with a robust sense of humor. Assuming this is not the case, are you training Lil Player to pop bands? Does he practice with Monopoly money? Was the "I like the strip clubs" T-shirt out of stock? And does the shirt come with a certificate of authenticity? Remind me to Google that august agency that provides this certification.

172

(to the man driving the nice luxury car with the license plate "Too Fly") If you still use the word *fly* to describe your coolness, you are not fly. If you have a license plate frame that says "Too Fly to Fly" you are that much less fly. I guess "Too Hype," "Too Dope," and "Too Fresh" were taken. But thanks for the trip back to 1989, bro.

173

I have come to the conclusion that all boys are equipped with two napkins at all times. Girls refer to these as "hands." Note that the boy napkins are rarely clean.

174

Physicians, there will be times when you have to explain abnormal lab results to a patient. It is best to sit down and talk to said patient face-to-face. It is bad to simply draw a yellow frowny face next to any lab values marked "Critical." It is actually worse to refer to the patient by the wrong name in writing next to the frowny face. And, yes, the patient's name was spelled correctly at the top of the page.

175

If you have a severe cough, a fever, chest pain, and shortness of breath, you may have pneumonia. Please note that this is not an appropriate time to smoke a cigarette to calm your nerves. And please remove the box of unfiltered nicotine sticks from your shirt pocket so I can examine your ailing lungs. Thank you.

176

To the hip-hop artist 2 Chainz, who wants a "big-booty girl" for his birthday: If you're making hit records and are appropriately compensated, shouldn't you be attracting ladies on other days? When I was a kid, rappers had enough skill to attract women on other days. Why should I fund your current small-booty-woman/no-woman lifestyle by purchasing your music?

177

Formfitting yoga pants are not appropriate attire for everyone—OK, fellas? I'm glad you are happy to see me.

178

To the person wearing the T-shirt emblazoned with the phrase "Don't sweat my swag!" OK, I will refrain from doing so. But, kind sir, what is the basis for your swag? As far as I can tell, it is based on being carbon based and oxygen requiring. Plus an overinflated sense of self-importance. My advice: acquire a marketable skill, pull your pants up, get a belt for said pants, and realize that self-respect is more than a fifteen-dollar T-shirt.

179

If your child was born during football season, your child's birthday party needs to be on a weeknight. Or you need to have the game on during the party. If neither of these options are feasible, tell said child his/her birthday is in February or August. Please—for the children.

180

If WebMD says you have [insert name of rare illness] and no physician, living or dead, can find evidence of said infirmity, then have WebMD do your referral and file the appeals necessary to have your insurance company pay for your specialist visit. Look—I'm on your side. But when the insurance company says no, and only then do you mention some vital piece of information needed for us to make your diagnosis, your blaming me for not being a soothsayer is not the best solution.

181

Why does Facebook think I will like the page Mobile Tans by Paige? Maybe they think I would prefer to be tan instead of dark skinned. I should go to a tanning salon and ask if they can make me tan colored. Maybe they just adjust the tanning bed to the "reverse" setting.

182

Coloring your hair can be a good way for you to accentuate your natural beauty. If you decide to dye your hair, I have some advice for you. Consider choosing only one color, or limit it to two. Glitter should be used sparingly. And please utilize shampoo. You are not a pleasant sight when your hair resembles a glittery porcupine at a gay-pride parade.

183

Running is a great way for you to get in shape. If you live in a warm-weather climate, staying hydrated is very important. Despite having that knowledge, I did not hydrate after my morning run. Now I'm kinda dizzy. <facepalm>

184

A few observations from the Original Greek Festival: Houston is a multicultural city. Greeks know how to cook. My kids know how to eat. Warm weather equals cleavage. Old people have more fun than young people—no pretense. Meat always tastes better on a stick. Houston is a great place to live. My kids are getting better at sharing. Kids are greater than college football.

185

I will not prescribe anxiety medications sight unseen over the weekend when you give a fake name and tell me that your family member committed suicide. Especially when that family member successfully committed suicide in the same fashion four months ago. Remember—fake name goes with fake voice, and you must change details of the story. Apparently drugs do not impart wisdom.

186

If my son plays cornerback and he ever lets anyone get five yards behind him *twice*, I'm putting him on Craigslist.

187

The morning-after pill does not prevent pregnancy if taken by the male. Also, taking antibiotics before having relations will not prevent pregnancy or STDs. Yes, I said pregnancy.

188

If you are diabetic, it is important to take your medications consistently as prescribed. Therefore, it is vitally important to make sure to get medications refilled BEFORE they run out. Since I have not renewed my clairvoyant license, it is not my fault that you ran out on a weekend. Maybe you should have tried the whole refill request thingy that is catching on with the kids these days. Now you are claiming this is an EMERGENCY, albeit an emergency that could easily have been anticipated and avoided Monday through Friday during business hours like 99% of my patients. I am going out on a limb here, but telling the pharmacist and physician that it will be our fault if something bad happens is like blaming us for your rudeness, pre-existing conditions, and non-traditional/unattractive haircut. And no, the pharmacy will not open early on a Sunday to accommodate your inability to look at a pill bottle and count to 2 on a Friday.**Calling on a weekend is fine. Answering the phone yelling at me before telling me your situation is not.

189

Whenever I have been told to throw my hands in the air, I have complied. I even waved them as if I don't care. But I did care, and I still do care.

190

(after the Astros lost their hundredth game one season) My son's quote of the day: "Maybe they need to try another sport."

191

If you're going to try to convince a doctor or pharmacist that you need drug refills earlier than expected, here are a few handy tips. Pick a drug that is not often sold by non-licensed, self-employed, untaxed pharmaceutical distributors named "Good Time". Saying that the drug was stolen or lost is so cliche, jazz up the story with fake police reports and made up diagnoses. In fact, just invent your own vocabulary to keep me entertained. Finally, ...if the event that made you take more medications occurred on Friday, but you asked for refills on the Wednesday before, it can bring your veracity into question. So double down on your story- you needed the extra medication because your dog died. Much like long term investing, a diverse portfolio is more likely to yield dividends. Unless the portfolio is made up of diverse types low yield investments.

192

I'm turning 40 next week. I know a man my age getting brain surgery for a tumor next week. You just never know what tomorrow is going to bring. I am going to walk to the next room- because I am able to walk.

193

(To the person who left the "gift" in the men's room at my office): The matches did NOT even come close to working. The can of Lysol next to the toilet is for this type of "emergency". Also, you have my permission to use the plunger next to the can of Lysol. I hope there is a CPT code for this procedure, since I had to use gloves.

194

If your child erupts in tears at the idea of taking a nap, your child needs a nap. The amount of tears is proportional to the necessity of the nap time. For instance, I am living in the Amazon Rain Forest. Ergo, nap time. If you start crying, too-you also need a nap.

195

Physicians, we understand that your job is important. Sometimes you just have to return a page during a meeting. One suggestion: if you are in a meeting full of physicians when you get paged, stand up, walk out of the room, THEN return the call. Your cupped left hand is not a sound proof barrier. By the way, all of us are glad Lil Johnny is doing his homework. Bonus points for having the "honking clown nose" ringtone for your text messages.

196

Not a Public Service Announcement, but it's pretty funny:

Me, to my Stage 4 cancer patient: Thanks for coming out today. It's good to see you.

Patient: It's good to be here. Hell, it's good to be awake!

197

The internet is a wonderful tool. When used wisely, the information superhighway is a road to good information. However, just because it is on the internet, it is not necessarily true. For instance, no matter what you looked up, if you are able to speak loud enough to make deaf people in Canada wince in pain, you are not suffering from a respiratory arrest or cardiac arrest. Also, neither of these conditions is cured by Xanax or Vicodin.

198

When using a public toilet, the first item of business is to check for the availability of toilet paper. Assuming you have skipped step 1, bring a 7 year old who is willing to get said item for you. And tell him that it is ok to give the toilet paper in denominations greater than 3 squares at a time.

199

To the insurance company who uses Fed Ex to send reimbursement checks: thank you for the $3.27 payment. Now I am only $1.50, 4 Chuck E. Cheese tokens, and 7 cereal box tops from world domination. Next time, could you send payment via direct deposit or US mail- and add the difference in postage to my reimbursement? If the check were for $50 or more, can you get Mr. Obama to hand deliver it, since you have so much extra money?

200

If you are going to call your doctor on a weekend about medication your dog ate, please call a physician you have seen in the past. Or a physician in a state you have at least visited. I guarantee that if you have never been to Texas, I did not write your original prescription. Also, if you have called the wrong physician, hitting the redial button will not make me the right physician, Einstein. But I do appreciate that you took the effort to change your voice and your story the second time. Well played, sir (who tried to pass himself off as a ma'am).

201

(To the person who came to the office an hour late for an appointment): I appreciate your gracious offer to wait until the other patients have been seen. You even pointed out that you would be willing to be seen during my lunch break! Despite that tempting offer, I politely declined, opting instead to follow my own medical advice by eating meals regularly. Don't get me wrong- I like my job and my patients. I just don't like hypoglycemia. ** By the way, when I eat lunch, I am still working.

202

A healthy breakfast is a great way to start your day. Generally, I am in favor of eating healthy. One exception to this rule is when you eat while driving. Especially when you are eating yogurt with a spoon while driving down 288. Judging by your weaving and obstructing behavior, it is also healthy to hold your steering wheel with at least one hand and look at the road while driving. And no, we were not all using out horns to say good morning.

203

(To the rap community): I am noticing a recurring theme among Hip-Hop artists. It seems as though many of you frequent strip clubs. You brag about spending enormous amounts of money so you can watch beautiful, elegantly clad women perform the Charleston or the Macarena (I am making an assumption, maybe they Waltz or 2 Step). And you think this makes you cool or trendy. To me, it says, "Despite having an enormous ego and large sums of money, I can not get women to have sex with me, unless I pay them. Then, they don't ACTUALLY have sex with me, I just kinda watch them jiggle." Since I can have women avoid sex with me for free, this seems like an unwise investment. Please let me know if I am misinterpreting the lyrics. Clap-Clap.

204

Sometimes in life, you have to make a difficult decision. You come to a fork in the road and you do not know which path to take. So here is some advice- if you have a child in your car and you have to get out of the car to enter any type of building-take the child with you. OK? If you disagree, please explain to me what on God's green Earth is in that building that is more important than your child. And, yes, I am ignoring the fact that if you need this message, that child shares your DNA. Mutations happen.

205

If I can see your drawers thru your pants, you're not wearing pants. May I suggest wearing clothing when going out? I'm going out on a limb here, but if I rocked that look at the office, I'd lose customers. And self-respect.

206

Jesus said that where 2 or more are gathered in his name, there will he be also. Apparently, get 10 or more, and play music, they will all wobble with it.

207

To my fellow Americans, the time has come for us to band together and rid America of the scourge that plagues us all. Until we address this issue we will never advance as a people. Can we please finish doing our hair before going out in public? You'd swear it is a requirement to wear rollers or a Do-rag. Did you know that actually finishing your hair looks better? That's why they wear finished hair in the movies and TV shows. And please, don't tell me you were in a hurry: we all know better. As an addendum, my mother just explained the baggy pants phenomenon: "I guess he really likes his underwear." If you don't need this help, please find someone to help. Thank you.

208

Picking up those items your wife asked you to pick up on your way home is an important way to strengthen the relationship. It is not as important as turning off the car when you are shopping, or taking your child out of said running and unlocked car. But I guess it's a start.

209

Here at Stanley Primary Care, we help people with a variety of medical issues. We understand that you may come in with GI issues that require use of the facilities here. We kindly ask that you inform a member of the staff if you need assistance or help cleaning up. And the plunger next to the toilet is available for use for non-staff members. Although I am a proficient amateur plumber and janitor, it is not my chosen profession. **Just ask for help. We want to help. We just don't want the next patient to be surprised.

210

Running is a wonderful way to exercise. Although I prefer to run outdoors, inclement weather sometimes forces me to use a treadmill. Unless the treadmill begins to produce thick plumes of smoke. Then I suggest running outside immediately.

211

(To the crestfallen young man pulled over on Beltway 8): You have my sincerest sympathy. I am sure that the police officer discriminated by choosing you for a citation. The fact that your car had the words "Street Lethal" emblazoned in an Old English script was probably just a coincidence. And I am sure that the flames on the side of your car symbolized the flames of justice that burn in thy soul. I felt your disappointment, amigo. But not your surprise.

212

(To the person wearing the t-shirt emblazoned with the sentence, "Awesome ends with ME!"): there is so much for me to say. Since awesome begins elsewhere, is it all used up just before it gets to you? Are you where awesome goes to die? Awesome begins with "awe" and has "so" in the middle- would you be offended if I said "so"? Loathsome ends with "me"- are you loathsome? Well, I am getting you a t-shirt that says "Mean begins with "ME!".

213

People, bargaining with your physician to allow you to eat junk food is not going to make the blood clot or bacteria avoid you. Even if you legitimately do not have time to eat right and exercise, the laws of physics and biology still apply to you. I do not have the ability to change that. And although I believe in prayer, the answer is often eat right and exercise.

214

I am a doctor. Note I did not say superhero or psychic. Therefore, if you call on the weekend, expect me to ask questions about your symptoms. If I care enough to ask, I'm trying to help you. And my ignorance of medical conditions you had before I was born does not imply I am uncaring. If I had a superpower, it would not be memorizing your medical history. I would opt for the ability to make you stop eating pork rinds by the gallon.

215

(To the lady at Chuck E. Cheese with the t-shirt saying, "if you were this awesome, you could be ME!"): Technically, that is true. Fortunately, I am not AS awesome as you. Thank you for the motivational message that inspires all of us to be our best. As for me, your self-confidence fills me with some awe.

216

Fellows, you never know when Cupid aims his arrow at your heart. It can even happen in your doctor's office. If you don't get her number, you can always give her your number. Or, leave a note on her car with your number. Please note, I said her car, not mine. I already have your number on the computer system and I have not used it yet. I do agree that I look good today.

217

Leg pain can be a sign of a medical emergency like a blood clot or infection. However, if the pain has been present since 1985, it probably is not an emergency. Asking your PCP to designate it so does not change that fact, even at 11 pm. Expecting an ER physician to fix your pain of 25 years in 30 minutes is like asking you to stop requesting a nurse to get you soda and Cheetos. And, no, we will not keep you here long enough to eat a breakfast sandwich. Oh, I stand corrected: sammich.

218

To the man with the Jazz Hands in the Galleria parking lot:
You clearly want a parking spot in the worst kind of way Yet,
your symphony of gesticulation seems to be in vain. And your
soliloquy of expletives has failed to move any unoccupied cars.
May I suggest other options, like leaving home earlier, or going to one of the 10 other garages with what I like to call "empty parking spaces"? Because stopping in the middle of the lot
isn't helping me or the occupants of the 6 cars behind me.

219

If you wear a shirt saying "Southern b!tc#es can't stand me", you're probably right. In all likelihood, people from many different regions and other genders can't stand you either. Does the back of the shirt say, "because they have common sense"?

220

Because I was asked, I will answer. Yes, smoking is bad for your lungs, too. Although it is good for my business, I can not recommend smoking for any medical reason.

221

If you come to a physician's office for ear pain, please adjust your wig and/or weave so that the physician can see your ear.

222

My son's quote of the day, "Do the Rockets practice?"

223

If you go to any self-respecting gym, and you are wearing a "Millionaire's Club" t-shirt that is holier than the Pope, you are not a millionaire. You are also not a member of any club that requires an invitation or hygiene. Therefore, the attractive female personal trainer is not showing you how to run- she is fleeing the premises.

224

Texting while driving is dangerous and reckless. However, when you see a police officer texting while driving, it is ironic, too. Should I have made a citizen's arrest?

225

If you do not look like Nicki Minaj, do not go out in public dressed like Nicki Minaj. Do not take the avertive gazes of all males as flirting, we're just trying to avoid eye contact. Also, I would like amnesia for Christmas.

226

Many grocery stores have self service areas. Self-service does not mean "stuff my jowled face with free food with my bare, unwashed hands". At least have the dignity to use the scoop thingy. Or attempt to hide your theft.

227

I would like to publicly apologize to the employee of (store x) for my offensive behavior. Normally, I self-serve, but my desired item was out of stock. I saw your logo'd polo and name badge and assumed I should ask you if said item was in stock. Taking that personal phone call let me know who was boss. By the way, Say hello to your baby mama for me. Your skill in passing me to a fellow employee who passed me to a fellow employee was admirable. Your smirk of glee as you declared that it was your break time filled all of us customers with joy as we shared your accomplishment You exhibited true grace and aplomb. Please note I did not use the word "co-worker", as neither of us want to associate you with work.

228

I understand that you would like to stop your medication that you take daily for high blood pressure. Sure, it controlled your symptoms and now you feel like you did before you started it. You had no side effects, and it was inexpensive. But you don't want to be dependent on medications "just in case it might be bad" and "it doesn't hurt to be safe". And God/your self-discipline/the dude on the infomercial said you can do this on your own. You even say you will "detox" from the medications. Can I make one request? Next time you give me the education I didn't get in med school, could you at least hide the pack of smokes? Or since tobacco is all natural, it's OK?

229

(just after the Trayvon Martin Case hit the news): I just had the most alarming encounter. I walk into an exam room in my office and BAM!! A person wearing a Hoodie. It turns out she's in her mid-80's, uses a walker, and it was a Cookie Monster hoodie, but still. She should have known better. Of course, she could say, "I was waiting in my doctor's office, when a Black guy wearing jeans just walks right in!! I was feeling threatened!! He walked right up to me, and even touched my chest! Of course, he's the doctor, and he touched my chest with a stethoscope, but still!!" Since my blue polo matches her Cookie Monster Hoodie, maybe we're both Crips? I gotta ask Geraldo Rivera about that. **She purposely wore a Cookie Monster Hoodie because she thought it was a form of protest humor. She got me to laugh.

230

(To the man with the license plate that reads "ME ME ME"): Unless you are really into musical scales, you might not be as clever as you think. When you are your own biggest fan, there is probably plenty of room on the old "ME" bandwagon. They say it`s lonely at the top, I guess the same can be said about your place in life, too. Thank you for informing the Greater Houston Area about your general awesomeness, bro.

231

(To the man on FM 518 with the large yellow sign stating "We buy your gold and silver!!!") : I am sure you are a man of your word and you believe in fairness and openness. Your Al Sharpton perm, Bill Cosby sweater, and NASCAR trucker hat indicate that you are a man of eclectic tastes and cosmopolitan demeanor. And the gold in your teeth shows that you know how to accessorize, too. I am going to trust you with as many heirlooms as I can find as soon as I get home.

232

When driving in heavy rain, it is imperative to drive with extra caution. Neither driving skills nor conversational abilities are enhanced when texting, driving, and rain are combined. Sometimes, due to poor visibility or mechanical failure, you may need to pull over and stop. Get these 2 steps in the right order: Please pull over before stopping. If that is not an option, use hazard lights. Unless you have super powers, your shaking fists of fury will not cause my car to magically start evasive actions. Lights would do that.

233

If your physician is unwilling to refill your addictive anxiety and pain medications during office hours, what makes you think said physician will refill said medications on weekends? I did not attend 4 years of college, 4 years of medical school, and 3 years of residency, so I could spend my free time helping you stockpile medications to sell to others for a profit. Somehow, no one ever runs out of blood pressure medications, nor do the infamous "two dudes" steal cholesterol medications on the weekends. It didn't help that when I said no, you questioned my manhood and medical acumen. Remember kids, drugs do not make you smarter.

234

Waiting in line at the Rodeo Carnival is a great place to teach a child manners and patience. It is not where you teach your child covert ops in order to cut in line. Lil Ninja isn't fooling anyone. It is not the place where your child's acting acumen will buy him a better spot in line. The fake tears moved all of us to yawn listlessly. Just slow down, enjoy the weather, and wait.

235

Jogging is a wonderful form of exercise. Unfortunately, injuries can and do occur. Rest is a marvelous tonic for injured joints. A word to the wise: if you injure your foot running a 6.2 mile race one day, running 6 miles the next day is not a good way to improve your symptoms. On the plus side, the painful, swollen ankle makes me forget about the foot pain.

236

High heel shoes at the Rodeo, in combination with inebriation, makes for an entertaining spectacle. On a related note, if that is your plan for the evening, might I suggest a cab and a tetanus shot? And keep those clothes on!

237

Lectures are an important aspect of the educational process. And thanks to PowerPoint and laser pointers, lectures are easier to prepare. If you are a lecturer with a laser pointer, I would like to offer advice. Assuming we can read, let us do so without pointing the laser in our eyes. If you are pointing at something- aim. Shaking the pointer at the whole slide does not help. And if the joke falls flat, just let it go, bro. Let it go...

238

Sometimes, people change phone numbers and do not inform others of the change. If you send an e-mail to your PCP asking why you did not get a phone call, and the office replies that the number we dialed is not the correct number, it is perfectly acceptable to send a reply with a new number. Or answer one of the 3 e-mails we previously sent. Or reply to the letter we mailed to your home address. I would like to request that the new number be your number, and not the number of a man with anger management issues. Thank you;-)**To clarify, the e-mail reply had the wrong number. When I dialed the wrong number, the person who I called was VERY unhappy that I called. I was, and am still, afraid to ask why.

239

As a small business owner, I know the value of good marketing. Yesterday, I found inspiration at Bucee's. A 2010 Chevy Impala was emblazoned with the logo of a local record label. The 24 inch wheels and Lambo doors were clear evidence of success and investment savvy. The heavy bass shaking the homemade-tinted windows is still rattling my ossicles. But what won me over- a bumper sticker of a UPC code with the phone number of said record label. I know I'm getting Lambo doors on the Accord. And I am buying their collection of gospel ballads and contemporary jazz albums.

240

A shiny car is like ExLax to a bird.

241

People, please hear me. Leggings are not pants. Especially when You are trying to squeeze your size 12 self into size 6 leggings. The elastic actually cried out for help. For the sake of the feet of dromedary mammals, wear pants that are pants.

242

Chest pain, when accompanied with elevations in blood pressure and palpitations, is an emergency. Therefore, if you experience these symptoms together, dial 911 and get to an appropriate emergency room. Calling your PCP for a direct admit on the weekend will not stop the blood clot or arrhythmia from killing you. And going straight to the medical floor may make you feel important, but that won't cure your potentially fatal condition. The ER is equipped for this. So when I say, "Hang up and dial 911" that means I care more about you living than being polite. Say it with me: Emergencies belong in the Emergency Room.

243

Why do Legos have an upper age limit? Like we're ineligible to play with them after age 14. Will the Lego Police get a warrant for my arrest?

244

A dash of fine cologne can enhance the appeal of a well groomed gentleman. However, a boatload of cologne, can suffocate a small child and singe the eyebrows of mortal men. Even if (ok, when) you have an odor that knocks leaves off trees, kills birds mid-flight, and disables military aircraft, extra cologne will not hide that pungent aroma. May I suggest soap, with a dash of water? With a side of clean clothes, of course.

245

I feel confident, based on her lyrics, that Nicki Minaj has seen more male genitalia than any urologist currently practicing at this time. She has also used all seven of George Carlin's forbidden words in one sentence.

246

(for the Dad behind me): All children are beautiful gifts from God. Including yours. Please do not take that gift for granted. If they continue to fall forward, I can not guarantee that I will be available to serve as a cushion and napkin. It's also OK to say excuse me.

247

Many of you have decided to dye your beautiful locks. Some of you have decided to get a weave or a ponytail. That's fine. A few suggestions for you. First, make sure that your hair color is one that has been seen on a human head before. I like toucans as much as the next guy, but wearing one is a bad idea. Next, pick one color to wear, I don't want to have a seizure. Hide the tag. And finally, feel free to match your technicolor dream coat of hair with your $250 purse, pajama bottoms and slippers while at Starbucks.

248

The elasticity of a six year old male bladder is directly proportional to the quality of the video game played. It is inversely proportional to the difficulty of the chore before him.

249

Reason # 421 to like kids: A three-year-old gets a scratch on his knee and want to come in. His mother tells him she can handle this. He keeps insisting he needs treatment for the knee- he's a boy. A week later, he gets a cough and high fever she brings him in. When I ask him to point to his chest so I can listen, he emphatically points to the scratch on his knee. So I listened. No wheezing. But now his knee is better.

250

If you are an insurance company and you design a prior authorization form that has the patient's name and date of birth on it- don't ask me if the patient is above the age of 4. I am fine with having someone looking over my shoulder with formulary decisions and cost calculations- just make sure said someone can count to 4.

251

The instructions "Ready, Aim, Fire!" apply to sharpshooters, snipers, and firing squad members. Fellas, you too can use this in daily life, even if you do not own a firearm. For instance, if you are using a public restroom- aim before firing. This can be applied to any bathroom procedures (1,2, or the rarely used #3- vomitus).

252

If you lose your medications, a doctor or pharmacist is not obligated to replace your medication. However, if you want early refills, here's some advice: Arrange to have your blood pressure medications lost/stolen at the same time. Keep your story of adventure and tale of woe concise and focused (I don't care if your cousin stole it). If you repeat the story, do not change important details like the name of the drug and the offending family member. Get the name right. Or get it wrong the same way each time. Also. Get my name right, too. And if we refused to fill the prescription during office hours, taking personal time after hours will not get old Dr. Stone here to call in your addictive prescription.

253

(To the man wearing the "MILF HUNTER" t-shirt): Given the number of Crucifix tattoos emblazoned on your arms, I am compelled to ask if you accurately represent the values espoused by the Savior. Thank you for informing ladies which ones meet your rigorous standards. Ladies without children, REJOICE!!!

254

If you play defense for a football team, your job is to tackle people. When you do so, you can walk back to the huddle. You do not need to act like you just had an epic orgasm while winning the lottery. You stopped a guy after a 3 yard gain. And you're down 26-0. Sit down, shut up, and make a tackle on 3rd down, Sparky.

255

Stanley Primary Care is open from 8 am - 5 pm. As much as I would like to accommodate patients before and after those hours, I am unable to do so. Therefore, when you call and tell the staff you will arrive a little after 5, even though you do not have an appointment, you can expect to be greeted by our lighted sign and Welcome mat. Asking for a favor works better than demanding it. Or at least offer to personally explain to all of the children of staff members why their parents are late picking them up.

256

Viagra will not help you attract the lady (or male) of your choosing. I repeat—it does not make you more desirable. Therefore, a lack of Viagra is not your particular problem. There's no cure for what you have. Fortunately, if this is a genetic problem, your genes will not likely be passed on.

257

The emergency-room physician cannot cure your mother of the affliction "old and tired." Nor can he or she cure "old and weak." Our time machine is broken. Sorry. Should've asked Santa for one.

258

Occasionally, as a patient, you will disagree with the treatment decisions made by a physician. You may decide to leave, against medical advice. When doing so, it is perfectly acceptable for you to leave the cup of urine you are holding in the exam room or bathroom. Or put the lid on tightly. But if you must leave, announcing it with "All y'all no good idiots" does not make us want to chase you down to provide better service. After all, apparently we're all idiots.

259

When you see a representative of the Salvation Army during the holiday season, it is polite for you to share in charitable giving. But do not be too ostentatious. For instance, if you try to put your money in the kettle and you miss, just pick up the money and put it in the kettle. But when you run into the sign and kettle at the same time, remember to put the kettle and the sign back where they belong. I think I hurt my shoulder too.

260

If you had appendicitis in the past and it was cured with an appendectomy, then you currently do not have appendicitis. Even if you looked it up on WebMD. And you brought the printout from WebMD. Just trust me. I took a few classes. So did the other doctors who told you that you do not have a repeat case of appendicitis. Perhaps you missed the part about the appendix not regenerating. Unless you're a starfish.

261

Sea lions are different from seals. To the man at the Houston Zoo who just educated my six-year-old son, I am glad you have found your true calling. How this charming ace zoologist does not have his own Christmas special on Animal Planet is beyond me. Oddly enough, neither my six-year-old nor my nine-year-old was impressed by your dissertation, and they continued to call the sea lion a seal.

262

If you have kids…

> Parent: Child, finish your dinner.
> Child: But I'm so full! Just saying *food* makes me ill. I cannot fathom eating another bite. Ever. Again.
> Parent: Well then, I guess none of us can go for ice cream.
> Child: <chomp, slurp>
> Parent: Let's get that ice cream.

263

Many doctors keep magazines in their waiting rooms to make people feel comfortable and to help them pass the time. Please note that this is not required reading. You can put the magazine down when your doctor is asking you questions regarding your chest pain, fever, or diagnosis of cancer. When you forgot to mention you actually are allergic to penicillin (because you were too busy reading a magazine), the medical assistant who asked the question is not at fault. Unless said magazine can write a prescription for the antibiotic you don't need for the sniffles that started yesterday, pay attention to the humans who are trying to care for you.

264

Holiday lights are a decorative symbol of the festivities and merriment of the season. Christmas lights look wonderful on trees, houses, and fences. Unless you are a tree, house, or fence, you do not need to wear a sweater with lights. Or music. And this announcement also covers the sweater vest.

265

Boys have bladders the size of walnuts. And they are just as elastic.

266

(This one is not humorous- this is actual good advice)

If your child has a fever of 103.7 at three thirty in the morning and you're on the fence about what to do, call your doctor. I'm not a fan of losing sleep, but that's what I signed up for. And I'd rather lose sleep than have you wait four to five critical hours that could lead to losing your child. That's why I have an answering service, pager, and cell phone.

267

Herman Cain is "at peace with [his] God" while Ndamukong Suh justified his arm stomp by saying that "the man upstairs saw what happened." Can we call a moratorium on guilty people hiding under God (or something kinda close to God) to throw us off the scent? Either come clean or just flat out deny. Either way, stop pulling the almighty and holy God into your "errors," "lapses in judgment," and "mistakes." God has more important things to do than to be your wingman. Please note Mother Teresa did not need to use this tactic.

268

(to the man playing twenty questions with the cashier at the Lego Store) They're Legos! Just stack them up, and make shapes and other stuff. He is not going home to play with you. He is not your personal Lego design concierge. He is not even one of the four other workers designated to answer these questions who happen to not be the only cashier in the store. Please purchase your items, monitor your child, who keeps asking to go potty, and move to the side. Thank you.

269

If you come to my office for diabetes, high blood pressure, or high cholesterol and you mysteriously can't find a way to meet your health goals, I have a request. Could you try to hide the fact that you're going to the Kentucky Fried Chicken in front of my office immediately after the visit? Drive around the block once. Maybe go to one of the eighteen other fast-food options within a three-mile radius of the office. But I know that you are not first going to the pharmacy.

270

Fellow Texans, the weather outside is getting colder and less humid. This means that you should dress in layers, wear scarves, and keep your heads covered. And for the love of God, buy some lotion. There was a serious ash attack at the office today people. I nearly had an asthma attack. Ashy Larry asked you to tone it down. So please apply some lotion, or bring one of those little vacuum cleaners to clean my office. Thank you.

Note: This does not apply to people with certain medical conditions. Only to people who just need lotion and then apologize for leaving messes in the office due to acute lotion deficiency.

271

(to the man who stopped at a red light and then, though the light was still red, drifted into the intersection while talking on his iPhone) Did you know that the person on the other end of the line will still be there when (if) you get to your destination? And, unlike me right now, that person will be happy you have arrived there safely. Although you may be a gifted conversationalist, I speak for all of us in saying that I do not wish to have fellowship with you while making a police report stating that it was not my fault. OK? Thanks. And you can put down the coffee too.

272

Testing different products before you make a purchase is often a good idea. I used the word "often" instead of "always" because trying many brands of antiperspirant in the store is the exception to the rule. Although it seems polite to replace the tested product, in practice it is setting a booby trap. I would not like to be behind this guy in the toothbrush aisle. And I did not shake his well-traveled hand.

273

(to the lady with the vanity license plate that read DE-LISH) No. Just no. You did not come as advertised. My appetite was not whetted. I am going on a diet. But you did make me look.

274

(On the day before Thanksgiving)

I am thankful for the contact high my patient just gave me.
Now I have the munchies.

275

Truly being a man is a responsibility. Extolling the virtues of one's own manhood shows immaturity. Doing so by hanging a metal replica of a large scrotum from one's trailer hitch shows a tendency toward overcompensation. If you want to impress me (and I do not want to be impressed), just take a picture of the boys and make a bumper sticker out of that. Otherwise, I will start putting metal replicas of a uterus, ovaries, and fallopian tubes on your trailer hitch. Or I just might get a bumper sticker that says "I like to display external genitalia" and put it on your vehicle. At least it would be honest, right?

276

When choosing between a breast augmentation and breast tattoos, get the surgery first. My apologies if the family member you're memorializing actually was a cyclops.

277

The beautiful lady at the bar is not stuck-up. Her average-looking friend is not a snob. And the plain-looking girl is not arrogant. It's you, buddy. Please consider a breath mint, matching clothes, a comb, and a personality that does not make Jesus say, "Um, not you—I meant everyone else."

278

(to the person with the "I [heart] VAG" bumper sticker) Thank you for the news update. As they say, honesty is the best policy. Clearly you honor ladies with your commitment to integrity and anatomy. Oh, and the ability to ignore other body parts. I am sure your mother is proud. And given your chosen medium of expression, I am sure it [heart]s you right back.

279

When opportunity knocks, be ready to answer. If you consider yourself a groundbreaking musician in the gospel/opera genre, you should be ready to offer your demo tape to anyone in the music industry who is ready to listen. Or to any doctor you see in the ER where you are seeking care. Please note that when offering to give out said demo tape, you should not say, "Um, I gotta get studio time first, but yeah, it's good. You can tell I got talent, right?" He did have something—just not a demo tape.

280

Chest pain is a common symptom, and occasionally it is a har-binger of a serious medical condition, like a heart attack, pneumonia, or a blood clot in the lungs. It is important that you provide your physician with a thorough history of your symptoms. It is also important that you pause in the history giving during the exam. Because we kinda can't hear your heart or lungs while you're talking. Plus, if you try to shout during the exam, the ensuing deafness makes it hard for us to hear your important body parts that you came to have us examine. On a related note, the EKG will be more accurate if you are not trying to sit up, walk, or rearrange the sticky things on your chest during the exam.

281

Exercise is a wonderful and effective way to prevent heart attacks and strokes. Sometimes we do not feel like we have time to exercise. However, the blood clots do not care if you have time to exercise. And do not ask me if I understand how hard it is to exercise. I do understand, but my empathy is not as useful as your dropping the biscuit, getting off the couch, and sweating. Please remember that these are not my rules; these are the rules that physics, chemistry, and biology gave us. For further questions, go to my fake website: www.dropthebiscuitandwalk.com.

282

When arriving to a ten o'clock church service at a quarter to eleven, your bestowing the icy death stare on a fellow parishioner for being seated in your unmarked seat does not reflect what Jesus would do. Nor will it cause those of us who were on time (or within forty-four minutes of being on time) to oversleep so you can hear the same sermon in *your* seat. But I guess my condescending smirk of derision might not be on the good Lord's list of responses. Good thing God forgives.

283

(to the man who owns the vehicle stopped on the shoulder of the freeway) Your grill guard, gangsta white walls, cone-shaped hubcaps, and classy decorative spare tire show that you have invested heavily in your vehicle. The ladies love a shiny car. The fact that you have parked involuntarily has given more of us the opportunity to bask in your chrome-inspired glory. If I may offer some advice, here are some other neat ways for you to accessorize the vehicle: a spare gallon of gas, a working exhaust system, a muffler, a windshield without a long crack, headlights (plural, not singular), and a substance I like to call "oil." Because the ladies love a car that can move them. Literally.

284

You know how Superman can see through everything but lead because of his x-ray vision? Well, I for one would not hang out with him. If he looked at me too much, I could be at risk for lymphoma or thyroid cancer. That being said, he could use it for good if he looked at criminals exclusively, used the radiation like a microwave to properly heat foods to a safe temperature, or used it like proton-beam radiation to cure cancer. If he used it to make grilled cheese sandwiches, I could risk cancer for that.

285

As most of us know, hygiene is a very important aspect of maintaining good health. Some of us are unable to practice good hygiene because of health issues or injuries. If that happens in the hospital, it is perfectly OK for you to inform the hospital staff of the accident. A good way to inform them is to use the call button. A not-so-good way is to hide the evidence and ask, "Do you smell something?" when someone walks by. The worst way is to tell the nurse's aide that the nurse "did number one on the floor—I swear!"

286

This week, I learned women can get prostrate cancer; not to correct patients who tell me their mothers died of prostrate cancer; there are bacteria that scare away other bacteria; beer does not cure vomiting; Burger King does not cure diabetes, heart failure, or cirrhosis; and if a four-letter word does not make a nurse call the social worker, a twelve-letter word does not work any better. And, no, I did not misspell "prostrate."

287

Soap, despite being a four-letter word, should not be treated as such. Please apply it liberally, with water. Then rinse, with water. Please pass this message along. Because it is less than universally known.

288

If everyone in the store knows your child is named Jimmie Joe and every item in the store bears Jimmie Joe's Cheeto-stained fingerprints, then Jimmie Joe needs Ritalin. It also means Jimmie Joe is too loud. Bonus tip: Jimmie Joe's issues are genetically and environmentally based.

289

God is not a waiter. He is not the almighty and holy One so that he can take your suggestions and orders and do your daily bidding. He left a book with instructions. Read it. He is smarter than you. He does not care if your football team wins or loses either. Note: If you have a different faith, that Almighty is also not a waiter. Please reference the statements above.

290

Sign seen at a local hospital: "Breathe deeply, and feel how you are like the earth." Since the earth is covered in salt water, dirt, and the excrement of animals, I will take short, shallow breaths.

291

Quote from a patient regarding teaching her kids not to smoke: "You can get cancer for free. Why pay six dollars a day for it?"

292

I realize that the baggy-and-saggy-pants look is not going away. I can live with that. But I would like to ask those who indulge in this attire to wear underwear that is clean, opaque (as opposed to translucent), and intact. In other words, make sure the only hole is in the front. Thank you.

293

Before you participate in any athletic endeavor, consuming a meal consisting of carbohydrates and protein can improve your performance. Assuming that the carbohydrates and protein do not come in the form of a Frito pie and Coca-Cola. At nine in the morning. Heck, why not just give the kid beer and cigarettes?

294

Individual ice chips do not cause hypothermia. You did not save the life of your loved one. You just wasted five minutes of our lives with your eloquent, heartfelt, and irrational exegesis on the scourge that is the ice chip (singular). I am eagerly awaiting your scholarly research on this topic.

295

They're called "nurses," not "butlers." It's OK to follow their advice. I do.

296

We fully understand and appreciate your concern that your loved one has not had as many bowel movements and ice chips as the patient in the next room. Acute ice insufficiency has been a pox on humankind for centuries. However, we have decided to concentrate on the lack of oxygen and heart function first. If you feel this is not in the best interest of your loved one, feel free to get a second opinion. And since the nurses alertly saved your loved one's heart from stopping, thank them instead of accusing them of being anti–bowel movement (or proconstipation).

297

Since smoking is prohibited in hospitals, you may need to step outside in order to partake in nicotinic bliss. If you are a patient in a hospital gown and you are male, it is a good idea for you to cross your legs. Not Indian-style, by the way. Or wear underwear. I'm good either way. It seems the females know this already. Although smoking can cause erectile dysfunction, it does not cause shrinkage.

298

(to the erstwhile young men who practice skateboarding in front of my office) Your consistency and diligence is laudable. Here's some advice for you. Thin pieces of plywood do not support 130-pound humans; therefore, they make poor ramps. And using that tree to support the plywood helps my business tremendously. Also, staring at cars does not make them avoid you. That's a Jedi mind trick—and you are not a Jedi. Finally, end your jumps by landing on the skateboard with the wheels on the ground. That way it keeps rolling forward with you and your skin. Happy landings.

299

I am not a smoker. Therefore, I do not have a light or a spare cigarette. Nor am I inclined to help you obtain them. This is especially applicable if you are a patient at MD Anderson Cancer Center. And you are on oxygen.

300

To the man wearing his doctor lab coat to the restaurant last night: Thank you for letting all of us know you were there to help and serve. Given the furtive looks you gave all of us, I could tell you were concerned for our well-being. Your medical degree was earned, much like your right to wear the jacket. That being said, you do not have to exercise said right all the time.

301

If you have a medical condition that has not been diagnosed by twelve other doctors, do not ask me to believe that none of them ordered any lab tests or x-rays. Also, do not expect me to make a diagnosis within fifteen minutes like House—it takes him a full episode. Finally, do not blame me for not diagnosing you before your appointment. I appreciate the fact that you have faith in my abilities, but accurate guessing without any information is not one of my abilities.

302

If the meeting agenda does not indicate a coherent plan or reason for the meeting, Dr. Stanley does not need to attend said meeting. My ability to keep this chair from hitting the ceiling is equaled only by the table's ability to keep my head from hitting the floor.

303

If you arrive at a place of business twenty minutes after the posted closing time, it is not "dumb luck." The business is closed because it was time for them to close. Had they known you wanted to be late, they would still be closed. May I suggest leaving your house on time?

304

Diabetic gastroparesis does not cause weight gain. Also, nausea due to this conditions is not normally treated by doughnuts, pretzels, mashed potatoes, or other carbohydrates.

305

(to the insurance company that sent Stanley Primary Care a check for ten cents) Next time, send blank sheets of paper. I can actually use blank pages of paper. Apparently you were unable to mail a swift kick to the groin or a raised middle finger. I'd call someone who cares, but I need fifteen more cents.

306

Walking a dog with friends is a great way to exercise. And, understandably, both humans and dogs need to rest. That being said, it is OK to pick a resting location that is not a private driveway. Also, using your death stare will not convince me to switch houses so that you can own my driveway. Finally, thank you in advance for removing the well-placed organic fertilizer from the lawn. Did Rover eat beans?

307

Physicians, remembering your patients' names will help you build therapeutic relationships with them. This is especially true when you're jogging and you see your patient walking around the neighborhood. Especially when you saw him in the hospital earlier this morning and he has not been discharged. Because it might be awkward if you cannot remember his name.

308

The answer to the question "What hurts?" should not involve an explanation about why you fear airplane flights, why dogs are good pets, and how we need to improve environmental regulation.

309

Sometimes we experience wardrobe malfunctions. When that happens, it is perfectly reasonable for us to repair our clothing with sewing kits. In fact, I saw a patient do just that in my office today. During the interview. And the examination. A job well done. But next time, keep the girls covered up during the entire repair.

310

Pharmacists and physicians recommend reading the drug information you are given with your medication. It is OK to read past the words "Call your doctor". And although I appreciate the trust you have in my opinion, I am not the Physician's Desk Reference. I am not going to say that you are the only person to get this particular side effect from this medicine after it has been prescribed millions of times. Especially when you have not taken the first dose.

311

There are some people who are blessed with a natural sense of rhythm. Others do not have that gift. Then there's the lady in the turquoise blouse in section 133 who can't quite master her timing with the rest of us at the ballgame doing the wave. Here's some advice. If the other, coordinated people in your section are sitting, stay seated. And feel free to grip that beer just a bit tighter.

312

(To the man blessing my son's 5-6 year old flag football team with Lil Wayne (uncensored, of course)): A hearty thank you. I like Weezy as much as the next guy. But I like sex, which I also do not display during my son's football practice. Crank it up to 11.

313

If you are a male and you are wearing jeans with a large, colorful bird stitched on one leg, you do NOT have street cred. And the ladies are not checking you out. Those smiles are from laughter.

314

Athlete's foot is a legitimate medical condition, often success-fully treated by over the counter medications. Interestingly enough, these medications are not deliverable by EMS person-nel. Nor do they deliver cigarettes. And in case you were won-dering, the word "athlete" is not used regarding this person in any other capacity.

315

Calling 911 for an unconscious stranger is an act of kindness similar to the Parable of the Good Samaritan. However, a bad Samaritan would neglect to give the location of the needy person. And please make sure that the unconscious victim is present when EMS does finally find the alleged location.

316

If Starbucks is your office, you should refrain from using the speakerphone. Especially when you talk loud enough for Helen Keller to ask you to be quiet. And for God's sake- the cup is empty- quit trying to use the straw, Mr. Slurpee.

317

(To the "man" wearing the t-shirt with the inscription "Certified Muff Diver Instructor"): I am sure you are as advertised, despite the unwashed hands and unbrushed teeth. I will google the name of said academy shortly. The saying goes- Those who can, do. Those who can't teach. I am sure you exemplify that.

318

(To the male of this species who evenly coated the toilet seat at the Houston Museum of Natural Science): Well played. Neither Picasso nor Rembrandt so thoroughly covered a canvas as you had. And your choice of medium and use of the color yellow was breath-taking. Literally.

319

If you need someone to visit you in the hospital, people named "Slim" who are worried about going to jail are not your best option.

320

Jesus can be in more than one place at one time. The ER staff can not. If you want to be seen by a physician immediately on arrival to an overflowing emergency room, bring your own doctor.

321

When you need to ask "Do you know who I am?", the answer is "no". And once you say who you are, we are not impressed.

322

If you are a patient advocate for a family member, the words "please" and "thank you" are appreciated. However, in order for those words to be effective, you should address hospital employees and not other patients. Also asking "Do you know my mama?" is not the best way for us to guess what treatment your family members need. The sign on the door does not say "Mind Readers".

323

Public, or shared computers are "shared". Failing to log out of your Facebook accounts can lead to pregnancy, engagement, increased libido, diarrhea, embarrassment, and me laughing. A lot. At you.

324

(From a lady in her 50's who was struggling with chemo-therapy): "I'll be here all week. Don't forget to tip the waiters! Remember, these jokes are better if you've had 2 drinks!!"

325

Being a good salesperson requires enthusiasm, people skills, and optimism. It also helps if you are in the right location. For instance, selling candy to diabetic patients is a bad idea. Selling it to them in an emergency room is worse. Asking complete strangers,"Whatcha in here fo'?" completes the trifecta. But the icing on the cake- a bad wig. Thank you.

326

Wear sunscreen. Unless you like sunburns and skin cancer. I mean, do you skip wearing an oven mitt because it's inconvenient? Why not skip hand washing? Wait, too many of y'all do that anyway. So please wear sunscreen!!!

327

(to the man wearing the all Black Dickies shirt/work pants combo and the black baseball cap at a suburban Starbucks): It is no longer 1988. Let NWA keep their image and style. Please note that 95 degree days, black clothes, and hot coffee will make you sweat profusely.

328

(To the man in the 95 Corolla with the $2,000 rims and midnight tint): Thank you for allowing the Texas Medical Center to be blessed by your musical choices. The ode to shaking buttocks was a fitting tribute to women and anatomy. I am sure your mother is proud of you. Thank you for promoting heavy usage of NSFW lyrics. True poetry speaks for itself; your amplifier spoke volumes as well.

329

These 2 happened on the same night.

1. Enjoying the benefits of crack and indulging regularly will not make the ladies swoon. Especially at the hospital where you are being treated for crack related maladies. Especially with the nurse who is treating you for crack related maladies. Of note, the subject of this PSA claimed to smoke $4,000 worth of crack daily. That's $167 per hour. At $10 per rock- one every 4 minutes (approximately). He might not be honest. He might be bad with math, too.

2. If you come to a hospital with complications related to your cocaine use, the doctor does not want to date you. Yes, a different cocaine addict is hitting on the workers here. And I was not left out.

330

Leaving your child by herself in the car with the AC running is a bad idea. It can lead to kidnapping, car loss, or a self-paced driving lesson.

331

If God is going to let us know he is going to end life on this planet, he's going to use better representatives than the current crop of lunatics.

332

Anyone else notice when an NBA player wants to "send a message" with a cheap shot, he always sends it to the smallest opponent? The message I get is, "I'm too much of a wimp to fight someone my own size." Please note that this does not apply to small opponents who are good at fighting like Delonte West, Rafer Alston, and Vernon Maxwell. Coincidentally, no one ever sent a message to Shaq.

333

If a flower delivery person brings flowers to your significant other, and you are wearing no pants, you don't have to come to the door. Granted, that maneuver did save him from me accepting a tip. I hope he was referring to money.

334

It is perfectly acceptable to pause when giving your health history to your provider. You can pause for the cardiac exam. You can pause for oxygen. You can pause so the provider can ask questions. Or even answer your question before asking 2 more entirely unrelated questions. Thank you.

335

Dear Best Buy customer, you are not negotiating the Treaty of Versaille. You are not fixing the deficit. You are not discovering a cure for cancer. You are saving $1 on a DVD. You may proceed to your car. Now.

336

God can cure your hypertension, but he would really like for you to follow at least SOME of his suggestions first. Also, medications can help, and they are not proof of disbelief.

337

Yelling or squinting will not make the ATM machine give you money. Having a bank account with a positive balance is a good alternative. Staring at me while I type this will not make the machine give you money. I've been in your shoes and it didn't work when I tried it, either.

338

Stanley Primary Care just got a check in the mail from a major insurer for 13 cents. Now we can finally buy that postage stamp. Please note, the check covered services for 2 patients.

339

When arriving to an emergency room stating you have been vomiting, we will not honor your request for mashed potatoes. We will also refrain from breaking into the closed cafeteria for said potatoes. Even if you say please.

340

Due to my inability to alter the time/space continuum, I will not be able to change what other physicians have done to you. I can not go back and prevent issues from occurring that have already occurred. If you feel malpractice has occurred, I can not reverse the actual course of history, even if you are polite or insistent. My apologies in advance.

341

You do not look good in leather pants. Shiny, yes. Good, no.

342

If you are over 50 and have an ample backside, please refrain from wearing hip hugger jeans. Remember, cleavage is best reserved for the front of the body.

343

When paging a physician on the weekend, it is perfectly acceptable to leave the correct number, actually answer when called, or check your voice mail before complaining that no one called back.

344

What's with action movies? Who can walk slowly when a 4,000 square foot building explodes 20 feet away- without getting thrown 50 feet or even getting a scratch from the wood, bricks, or nails flying around? AND their hair stays straight! Puh-leeze.

345

I just saw a promo for the Grammys. I am 38 years old and I have 2 children. Therefore, I have no clue who these performers are. Congratulations Mom and Dad, I am you.

346

An observation: When European soccer players are injured, the trainers pull out a can of magic elixir spray. Doesn't matter if they have a scratch, exposed bone, or rabies. Works every time. Where can I order a can? And then can I "Open a can" on my patients?

347

(To the American Idol contestants who don't make it and their lives are now a flaming pile of poo): Can I ask a question? DID ALL OF THE SCHOOLS CLOSE? If not, attend one of them, and get a job.

348

Stanley Primary Care does not provide narcotics on the weekend for the following situations: can't get a ride to the office but can get a ride to the pharmacy, didn't take the first medication I prescribed, having a "delicate constitution", having a normal MRI read by "those people who can't read MRIs", calling after hours, and asking me to wait by the fax after hours on a Friday to check labs someone else ordered. To the patient who hit all of these points today, that sort of drive and initiative is appreciated. It went unrewarded today, but keep up the good work!

349

If you are an overweight, underendowed humanesque male, please do not wear skinny jeans. Baggy jeans and slacks are viable options. Thank you.

350

If you absolutely must clip your fingernails, it is OK for you to wait until after you have left your doctor's exam room. Or even wait until the doctor is not in the room. Or at least pick up the clippings. Thank you.

351

I keep asking myself, Why do people refuse to take medications that have a 0.001 percent chance of hurting their livers, while they eat fifty-pound bags of salty pork rinds and drink cases of beer?

352

According to the form letter I just opened, the august body known as the International Association of Healthcare Professionals has approved my status as a "Top Doctor". I will be "spotlighted" in the "renowned" publication: "The Leading Physicians of The World". That's right people, Earth! Even though I've never heard of this group or this publication, I am sure it's legitimate and I should rush to send in the reply card. I think this is from the patient who called this weekend asking for pain meds.

353

OMG! Apparently, the world was not enough. According to this random fax, my 2011 Patients' Choice Award is now available. For $159 (plus $12.90 shipping and handling), I can have a plaque WITH A SEAL stating I am one of the best 5% in the nation. But since I got the planet locked up yesterday for free, I'll pass. If I'm one of the top 5% of doctors in America, it's time for all of us to move to a country with doctors who are perceived to be less gullible.

354

Excerpts from a conversation with a woman who processes appeals claims for prescription medication coverage. Keep in mind the prescription is a common birth control pill:

Her: I see she was given "XYZ" medication? Do you know what that is?

Me: It is the generic birth control pill, in fact, it is the generic of the pill she is taking.

Her: I wish I could look stuff like that up....

Me: Me, too. That would help right now.

Me: She takes 28 pills every month.

Her: Why? It should be 30, THAT'S her problem.

Me: Actually, most birth control pills are prescribed 28 days at a time. Monthly cycles are normally 28 days long.

Her: Really?

Me: (shaking my head)

Me: She takes this regimen because she had excessive bleeding and needed a transfusion with the other regimen.

Her: "So she took the medication for 3 weeks, then she bled to death and needed some blood."

Me: No, actually, she lived. That's why she still takes medications.

355

Conversation with insurance company regarding an MRI of the brain:

Insurance person (IP)- Have you treated this patient for this for more than a month?

Me- (scrolling through the chart) Yes, since February of last year.

IP- (sounding upset) So has it been at least a month?!?

Me- (counting to 1 in my head to make sure my math is correct) Yes, sir.

IP- Does the patient have a brain tumor?

Me- Yes, the diagnosis on the requisition is (withheld for privacy reasons- but many of you would recognize this as a brain tumor). Which is a type of brain tumor.

IP- Well, I'm not supposed to know that! Ooooh, but it does sound serious.

Me- Um, yeah. That's why we ordered the MRI. (deep sigh)

356

Written on Thanksgiving Day 2015

I am so thankful to have good friends and family. And a special thank you to the people who do not have a holiday today because they are serving the public- military service people, EMS, police, fire fighters, and hospital personnel (yes doctors and nurses, AND the numerous support staff we take for granted). Thank you all.

357

Written later on Thanksgiving Day 2015

I am also thankful for the race volunteer or participant who found my lost car key and turned it in. And thanks to the volunteers at lost and found who had a hearty laugh with me and at me.

358

Not a PSA- an emotional moment that is very common

Very difficult and emotional start to today. I had the opportunity to talk to a person in her last stages of life. I've done it before, and I'll do it again. It's as much a part of my job as joking with two-year-olds to get them to say "Aaaaah." Except it is not fun—and it's hard, it's rewarding, it's frustrating, it's liberating, and it's really, really sad. You want to get that last hug and those last words right, even though you know just showing up and being present is enough. I guess what I'm saying is this: Some days, doing the right thing can be easy and hard at the same time. Every day, it's important for you to be with the people around you—family, friends, acquaintances, strangers, and coworkers. Now go forth and give hugs to the living people around you.

359

Reason #3,298 to love sports: A man came to my office today wearing a New Orleans Saints stocking cap. It was a warm day, but the man was cold. This was probably because of the eighty pounds he had lost in the previous five months. Thanks, cancer. He was about to have a surgery involving the removal of his two most precious assets, and he was already using a tube and a bag to collect his urine. He was worried about another surgery. He was worried about bodily functions we take for granted. He was worried about just living, with or without the boys or the bag o' pee. Another patient who was a complete stranger to the man walked into my office, looked at the emaciated man carrying his own waste, and exclaimed, "Geaux Saints! We'll get 'em next year!"

And they exchanged a perfectly choreographed high five followed by the handshake hug.

Gotta love hope.